Tea Parties

AROUND THE WORLD

Tea Parties

AROUND THE WORLD

Globally Inspired Teatime Celebrations

hm | books

EDITOR *Lorna Reeves*

GROUP CREATIVE DIRECTOR *Deanna Rippy Gardner*

ART DIRECTOR *Cailyn Haynes*

ASSOCIATE EDITOR *Britt E. Stafford*

SENIOR COPY EDITOR *Rhonda Lee Lother*

EDITORIAL ASSISTANT *Katherine Cloninger*

STYLIST *Courtni Bodiford*

CREATIVE DIRECTOR/PHOTOGRAPHY
Mac Jamieson

SENIOR PHOTOGRAPHERS
John O'Hagan, Marcy Black Simpson

PHOTOGRAPHERS *Jim Bathie,*
William Dickey, Stephanie Welbourne Steele

ASSISTANT PHOTOGRAPHER *Caroline Smith*

SENIOR DIGITAL IMAGING SPECIALIST
Delisa McDaniel

DIGITAL IMAGING SPECIALIST *Clark Densmore*

FOOD STYLISTS/RECIPE DEVELOPERS
Laura Crandall, Janet Lambert, Vanessa Rocchio, Jade Sinacori

hoffmanmedia

CHAIRMAN OF THE BOARD/CEO
Phyllis Hoffman DePiano

PRESIDENT/COO *Eric W. Hoffman*

PRESIDENT/CCO *Brian Hart Hoffman*

EXECUTIVE VICE PRESIDENT/CFO *Mary P. Cummings*

EXECUTIVE VICE PRESIDENT/OPERATIONS
& MANUFACTURING *Greg Baugh*

VICE PRESIDENT/DIGITAL MEDIA *Jon Adamson*

VICE PRESIDENT/CULINARY & CUSTOM CONTENT
Brooke Michael Bell

VICE PRESIDENT/SHELTER CONTENT *Cindy Smith Cooper*

VICE PRESIDENT/ADMINISTRATION *Lynn Lee Terry*

Hoffman Media
1900 International Park Drive, Suite 50
Birmingham, Alabama 35243
hoffmanmedia.com

ISBN 978-1-940772-53-0
Printed in China

ON THE COVER: France, pages 32–45
ON THE BACK COVER: Apricot-Lavender Scones, page 37

Contents

Introduction

THE WONDERFUL CUSTOM OF AFTERNOON TEA may have been popularized by the British begining in the 19th century, but the joy of taking tea endures to this day and transcends national barriers. While tea is the most-consumed beverage globally (after water) and the plant it comes from grows in more than 64 countries, how people drink their tea and what they eat with it, however, vary from place to place.

Celebrate tea's international roots with ten menus for afternoon tea inspired by the cuisines and cultures of Australia, China, France, Japan, India, Morocco, The Netherlands, Russia, Scotland, and South Africa. Each course of these inventive menus is accompanied by tea pairings, which in some way reflect the country's tea customs. So they can be enjoyed warm, scones, which highlight iconic flavors, are presented as a first course in six of the menus. But for countries colonized or influenced by the British Empire, tea sandwiches or other savories are instead served first, with scones and sweets following as second and third courses, respectively.

Beautifully appointed tables, many decorated with china made in the various countries featured, incorporate national colors, native flowers, or other appropriate touches to fully capture the regional ambiance and to set the perfect stage for your teatime guests to join you for an international culinary tour that will not require a passport.

"Each cup of tea represents an imaginary voyage."

—Catherine Douzel

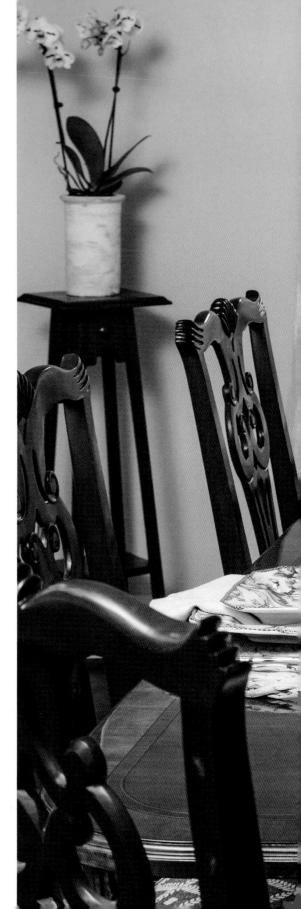

Australia

Although fluffy koalas, adorable wallabies, and the impressive Sydney Opera House might very well be some of the most iconic symbols of the Land Down Under, teatime is also an important part of Australia's culture. While tea growing only began here in earnest in the mid-20th century, tea drinking was introduced in the late 1700s by the British during their colonization efforts. Weddings and similar joyous events still are celebrated with tea, as are more somber occasions, such as funerals. Whatever the circumstances, Australians will often say that "a nice cup of tea" makes everything better.

Afternoon tea is served at posh restaurants and classic tea houses in major metropolitan areas but is equally prevalent in smaller towns. Fashioned similarly to the British style, a menu for an Australian teatime might include favorites, like savory sausage puffs, along with traditional tea sandwiches, such as cucumber. Scones follow secondly before a final course of local delicacies like coconut-covered lamingtons and Anzac biscuits. A table set with pretty china, like 222 Fifth's "Adelaide," and a selection of teas grown in the Land Down Under to accompany each course are lovely touches for any Aussie-inspired teatime.

The
MENU

SAVORIES
Herbed Cucumber Tea Sandwiches
Sausage Puffs
Prawn-Avocado Cocktails
*Green Tea &
Australian Lemon Myrtle*

SCONE
Damper Scones
Earl Grey Black Tea

SWEETS
Mini Mango-Kiwi Pavlovas
Lamingtons
Anzac Biscuits
Premium Blend Black Tea

*Tea Pairings by Madura of Australia,
+61 2 6670 6000, maduratea.com.au*

> *"My mother, along with all the other Australian mums since and prior, made sure we understood that we were supposed to drink tea."*
>
> —Kerry Vincent, Australian-born television host and award-winning cake designer

Herbed Cucumber Tea Sandwiches
Makes 16

4 ounces cream cheese, softened
1 tablespoon finely chopped fresh mint
1 tablespoon finely chopped fresh dill
⅛ teaspoon salt
⅛ teaspoon ground black pepper
⅛ teaspoon ground caraway seeds*
12 very thin slices firm white sandwich bread
48 very thin slices English cucumber
Garnish: fresh mint sprigs

• In a medium bowl, beat together cream cheese, mint, dill, salt, pepper, and caraway seeds with a mixer at medium-high speed until combined.
• Spread an even layer of cream cheese mixture onto bread slices. Lay 6 cucumber slices on a bread slice, shingling to fit. Place another bread slice, cream cheese side up, on top of cucumbers. Lay 6 cucumber slices on second bread slice, shingling to fit. Cover with a bread slice, cream cheese side down, to create a triple-stack sandwich. Repeat with remaining ingredients to create a total of 4 triple-stack sandwiches.
• Using a long serrated bread knife, trim and discard crusts from sandwiches. Cut each sandwich into 4 squares. Serve immediately, or cover with damp paper towels, place in a covered container, and refrigerate until serving time.
• Just before serving, garnish each tea sandwich with a mint sprig, if desired.

Using an electric spice grinder or a mortar and pestle, grind whole caraway seeds before use.

Sausage Puffs
Makes 24

½ (17.3-ounce) package frozen puff pastry,
    slightly thawed
1 tablespoon ketchup
6 (4-inch) pieces cooked beef sausage
1 large egg
1 tablespoon water
1 teaspoon sesame seeds

• Preheat oven to 400°. Line a rimmed baking sheet with parchment paper.
• Let puff pastry thaw just enough to be able to roll up and encase filling. (It should still be cold and firm.)
• On a lightly floured surface, unroll puff pastry sheet. Using a rolling pin, roll out puff pastry until smooth. Using a sharp knife, cut puff pastry into 6 rectangles.

Brush each rectangle lightly with ketchup, leaving a ½-inch border around edges. Place a piece of sausage on top of ketchup. Starting at one long side, roll up pastry rectangle firmly and evenly, tucking ends under. Repeat with remaining ingredients. Place sausage rolls 2 inches apart on prepared baking sheet.
• In a small bowl, whisk together egg and 1 tablespoon water. Brush sausage rolls with egg mixture. Sprinkle with sesame seeds.
• Bake until pastries are golden brown, 13 to 15 minutes. Let cool slightly. Using a serrated knife, cut each pastry into 4 (1-inch) pieces. Serve warm.

Prawn-Avocado Cocktails
Makes 8

4 cups water
1 tablespoon Old Bay seasoning
8 large fresh prawns, peeled and deveined (tails left on)
1 cup mashed avocado
¼ cup crème fraîche
4 teaspoons fresh lemon juice
4 teaspoons Dijon mustard
½ teaspoon salt
¼ teaspoon ground black pepper
Garnish: lemon slices, fresh baby arugula

• In a small saucepan, bring 4 cups water and Old Bay to a boil over medium-high heat. Remove from heat, and add prawns. Cover and let stand for 5 minutes. Remove prawns, and place in a bowl with water and crushed ice to chill. Pat prawns dry with paper towels.
• In a medium bowl, vigorously whisk together avocado, crème fraîche, lemon juice, mustard, salt, and pepper until creamy.
• Divide avocado mixture among 8 mini cocktail glasses. Top each glass with a chilled prawn.
• Garnish with lemon slices and arugula, if desired. Serve immediately.

resembles coarse crumbs. Add 1 cup milk and ½ cup water, stirring until mixture comes together.
• Turn out dough onto a lightly floured surface, and knead gently 4 to 5 times. Using a rolling pin, roll out dough to a 1-inch thickness. Using a 2¼-inch fluted round cutter, cut 11 scones from dough, rerolling scraps as necessary. Place scones 2 inches apart on prepared baking sheet.
• In a small bowl, whisk together egg and remaining 1 tablespoon milk. Using a pastry brush, brush tops of scones with egg wash.
• Bake until edges of scones are golden brown and a wooden pick inserted in centers comes out clean, 13 to 15 minutes. (The bottoms of the scones should sound hollow when tapped.) Serve warm.

Mini Mango-Kiwi Pavlovas
Makes 16

3 large egg whites
1½ cups fine sugar
¼ cup boiling water
1 teaspoon distilled white vinegar
1 teaspoon vanilla extract
⅛ teaspoon salt
1 tablespoon sifted cornstarch
1 cup cold heavy whipping cream
1¼ cups diced fresh mango
1¼ cups diced kiwi

• Preheat oven to 250°. Line 2 rimmed baking sheets with parchment paper. Using a pencil, draw 8 (3-inch) circles onto each parchment sheet; turn parchment over.
• In the bowl of a stand mixer fitted with the whisk attachment, beat together egg whites, sugar, ¼ cup water, vinegar, vanilla extract, and salt at medium speed until stiff peaks form, approximately 15 minutes. Add cornstarch, beating until incorporated. Transfer mixture to a piping bag fitted with a medium open-star tip (Wilton #21).
• Starting in center of each traced circle, pipe concentric circles of meringue mixture outward until each drawn circle is filled. Pipe 1 to 2 extra layers onto perimeters to form a rim around the edge of each circle.
• Bake for 1 hour. Turn oven off, and let meringues stand in oven for at least 2 hours or overnight. (This helps meringues continue to dry and form a crispy shell.) Store until needed at room temperature in an airtight container with layers separated with wax paper.
• In a medium bowl, beat cream with a mixer at high speed until soft peaks form. Divide whipped cream among meringues (pavlovas), and top with mango and kiwi. Serve immediately.

Damper Scones
Makes 11

4 cups self-rising flour
1 teaspoon salt
2 tablespoons unsalted butter
1 cup plus 1 tablespoon whole milk, divided
½ cup water
1 large egg

• Preheat oven to 425°. Line a rimmed baking sheet with parchment paper.
• In a large bowl, whisk together flour and salt. Using a pastry blender or 2 forks, cut in cold butter until it

HOW TO MAKE
PAVLOVAS

on page 130

Lamingtons
Makes 16 cakes

½ cup unsalted butter
¾ cup plus 2 tablespoons granulated sugar
2 large eggs, at room temperature
1½ cups all-purpose flour
1½ teaspoons baking powder
¼ teaspoon salt
½ cup whole milk, at room temperature
¾ teaspoons vanilla extract
4 cups minced dried unsweetened coconut
1 cup strawberry preserves
Chocolate Glaze (recipe follows)
Garnish: fresh strawberry halves

• Preheat oven to 350°. Spray a 9-inch square baking pan with cooking spray. Line pan with parchment paper, letting excess extend over sides of pan. Spray parchment with cooking spray.
• In a large bowl, beat together butter and sugar with a mixer at medium speed until fluffy, 3 to 4 minutes, stopping to scrape sides of bowl. Add eggs, one at a time, beating well after each addition.
• In a medium bowl, whisk together flour, baking powder, and salt. In a liquid-measuring cup, stir together milk and vanilla extract until combined. With mixer at low speed, gradually add flour mixture to butter mixture alternately with milk mixture, beginning and ending with flour mixture, beating after each addition just until combined. Pour batter into prepared pan, spreading to create a level surface. Tap pan on counter to release air bubbles.
• Bake until a wooden pick inserted in center comes out clean, 23 to 25 minutes. Let cool completely in pan.
• Place coconut in a shallow pan. Set aside.
• Using excess parchment as handles, remove cake from pan, and place on a cutting surface. Using a serrated bread knife, trim and discard edges from cake. Cut cake into 16 squares. Cut cake squares in half horizontally.
• Spread a layer of strawberry preserves onto bottom halves of cake squares. Cover with top halves of cake squares.
• Place cake squares on a wire rack set over a rimmed baking sheet. Pour warm Chocolate Glaze over each cake square, using a small offset spatula, if necessary, to spread glaze to cover top and sides completely. (Place bowl back over saucepan of simmering water, if necessary, to keep glaze pourable.)
• Place each chocolate-coated cake square in coconut, gently sprinkling and pressing coconut onto sides and top of cakes. Set on a wire rack to dry. Store cakes in an airtight container at room temperature for up to 3 days.
• Just before serving, garnish each with a strawberry half, if desired.

Chocolate Glaze
Makes 2¾ cups

3 tablespoons salted butter
⅓ cup natural sweetened cocoa powder
½ cup whole milk
4 cups confectioners' sugar

• In a large heatproof glass or metal bowl placed over a large saucepan of simmering water, melt butter. Add cocoa powder, whisking until a smooth paste forms. Add milk and confectioners' sugar, whisking and cooking until glaze is creamy, smooth, and pourable. Remove bowl from heat. Use immediately.

Anzac Biscuits
Makes 24

1 cup all-purpose flour
1 cup old-fashioned oats
1 cup dried unsweetened coconut
½ cup granulated sugar
½ cup unsalted butter, melted
1 tablespoon golden syrup
1 teaspoon baking soda
2 tablespoons boiling water

• Preheat oven to 350°. Line a rimmed baking sheet with parchment paper.
• In a large bowl, whisk together flour, oats, coconut, and sugar. Add melted butter, stirring well.
• In a small heatproof bowl, stir together golden syrup and baking soda. Add 2 tablespoons boiling water, stirring well. Add syrup mixture to oat mixture, stirring until a dough forms.
• Using a levered 1-tablespoon scoop, drop dough 2 inches apart onto prepared baking sheet. Using bottom of a glass, flatten dough portions to an even thickness.
• Bake until biscuits (cookies) are crisp and dark golden brown, 15 to 20 minutes. Transfer biscuits to a wire rack, and let cool to room temperature. Store in an airtight container at room temperature until ready to serve.

Because they were sturdy enough to withstand shipping without spoiling, Anzac biscuits were sent to soldiers serving in the Australian and New Zealand Army Corps (ANZAC) during World War I. Australian sugar artist and television personality Kerry Vincent provided the recipe that appears here and has been handed down through her family. "My grandfather and his four brothers served and received care packages from home with these biscuits, which were beloved because they easily lasted six weeks at sea," she says. Kerry also contributed the recipe for the pavlovas (page 16), which are her favorite teatime treats.

China

With a tea history dating back approximately 5,000 years, China is renowned as the birthplace of tea. Shennong, its mythical ruler at the time, is said to have discovered that the leaves of the *Camellia sinensis* (the tea plant) were suitable for steeping and that the resulting infusion was calming, restorative, and refreshing. Over the centuries, the Chinese have mastered the production of all six types of tea—white, green, yellow, oolong, black, and dark. While tea is cultivated in 18 provinces plus the autonomous region of Tibet and the municipality of Chongqing, certain areas, like the Wuyi Mountains of Fujian and the towns of Puerh in Yunnan and Long Jing in Zhejiang, are especially famous for their teas.

Celebrate China's many contributions to the tea-drinking world with an afternoon tea that draws inspiration from dishes that are often served for dim sum. Meaning "heart's delight," dim sum is fare served at tea houses in petite portions, such as pot stickers, steamed buns, and spring rolls. Our teatime menu also includes a first course of warm scones laced with honey and ginger and a final course of sesame balls, red bean paste cookies, and pineapple cookies.

The
MENU

SCONE
Honey-Ginger Scones
*China Cangyuan Yunnan
Organic Black Tea*

SAVORIES
Shrimp Spring Rolls
Vegetable Steamed Buns
Pork Pot Stickers
San-Xia Cloud & Mist Green Tea

SWEETS
Sesame Balls
Red Bean Paste Cookies
Pineapple Cookies
Goddess of Mercy Oolong Tea

*Tea Pairings by Simpson & Vail,
800-282-8327, svtea.com*

Honey-Ginger Scones
Makes 12

2 cups cake flour
1 tablespoon baking powder
½ teaspoon salt
¼ cup cold salted butter, cubed
3 tablespoons chopped crystallized ginger
1 cup heavy whipping cream, divided
¼ cup honey
1 egg yolk
Garnish: chopped crystallized ginger

• Preheat oven to 350°. Line a rimmed baking sheet with parchment paper.
• In a large bowl, whisk together flour, baking powder, and salt. Using a pastry blender or 2 forks, cut in cold butter until it resembles coarse crumbs. Add crystallized ginger, stirring to blend.
• In a small bowl, whisk together ¾ cup cream, honey, and egg yolk. Add cream mixture to flour mixture, stirring until mixture is evenly moist. (If dough seems dry, add more cream, 1 tablespoon at a time.) Working gently, bring mixture together with hands until a dough forms.
• Turn out dough onto a lightly floured surface. Using a rolling pin, roll out dough to a 1-inch thickness. Using a 2-inch fluted round cutter, cut 12 scones from dough, rerolling scraps once. Place scones 2 inches apart on prepared baking sheet. Brush tops of scones with remaining ¼ cup cream.
• Garnish top of scones with crystallized ginger, if desired.
• Bake until edges of scones are golden brown and a wooden pick inserted in centers comes out clean, 14 to 16 minutes. Serve warm.

HOW TO MAKE
SPRING ROLLS
——————
on page 128

Shrimp Spring Rolls
Makes 12

1 tablespoon soy sauce
1½ teaspoons rice wine vinegar
1 tablespoon plus 1 teaspoon cornstarch, divided
¼ teaspoon ground black pepper
½ cup (7 ounces) peeled and deveined medium
    fresh shrimp, chopped
1 tablespoon vegetable oil, divided
1 green onion, chopped
1 tablespoon minced fresh garlic
2 cups coarsely grated Napa cabbage
1 cup coarsely grated carrots
1½ teaspoons oyster sauce
¼ cup water
12 spring roll wrappers
Vegetable oil, for frying

• In a small bowl, whisk together soy sauce, rice wine, 1 teaspoon cornstarch, and pepper. Add chopped shrimp, and let marinate for at least 10 minutes.
• In a large skillet, heat 1½ teaspoons oil over medium heat. Add marinated shrimp, and cook until pink and firm, approximately 1 minute. Remove from skillet, and set aside. Clean skillet.
• In the same skillet, heat remaining 1½ teaspoons oil over medium heat. Add green onion and garlic; sauté until fragrant, approximately 30 seconds. Add cabbage and carrots; cook until carrots are slightly soft, approximately 2 minutes. Add cooked shrimp and oyster sauce, stirring to combine. Spread filling onto a sheet pan. Refrigerate until chilled.
• In a small bowl, stir together ¼ cup water and remaining 1 tablespoon cornstarch.
• Keep wrappers covered with a damp towel to prevent drying out. Place a spring roll wrapper, shiny side down with a corner pointed toward you, on a clean surface. Place 1 to 1½ tablespoons shrimp filling on corner closest to you. Fold corner tightly over filling. Fold left side in tightly, making sure not to leave any space, and roll once away from you. Fold right side in tightly, and roll again, keeping edges straight and even, until you reach top corner. Using your fingertip, brush edges of top corner with cornstarch mixture. Fold top corner to close roll, and place on a platter, seam side down. Cover with a damp towel. Repeat with remaining shrimp filling and remaining wrappers.
• In a wok, pour oil to a depth of 2 inches, and heat over medium heat until a deep-fry thermometer registers 350°. Working in batches, carefully slide spring rolls into hot oil, a few at a time. Fry, turning occasionally, until golden brown, approximately 3 minutes. Let spring rolls drain on a wire rack. Serve hot.

Vegetable Steamed Buns
Makes 20

1 baby bok choy
1 tablespoon vegetable oil
½ cup finely diced shiitake mushrooms
1 cup coarsely grated Napa cabbage
½ cup coarsely grated carrots
4 green onions, chopped
2 tablespoons plus 1 teaspoon granulated
  sugar, divided
1 teaspoon soy sauce
1 teaspoon sesame oil
1 teaspoon oyster sauce
1¼ teaspoons salt, divided
¼ teaspoon ground black pepper
⅓ cup finely diced daikon radishes
¾ cup warm water (100°)
1½ teaspoons instant yeast
2⅓ cups plus 1 tablespoon all-purpose flour

• Bring a large pot of water to a boil over medium-high heat. Add baby bok choy; cook for 10 seconds. Transfer to an ice-water bath to stop the cooking process and chill. Strain bok choy, squeezing out as much water as possible. Using a sharp knife, finely chop bok choy. Transfer to paper towels to let drain.

• In a large skillet, heat vegetable oil over medium heat. Add mushrooms; cook, stirring occasionally, until fragrant, approximately 3 minutes. Transfer to a medium bowl, and set aside. In same skillet, cook together cabbage, carrots, and green onion until carrots have softened, approximately 2 minutes, stirring occasionally. Add cabbage mixture to mushrooms. Let cool completely.

• In a medium bowl, stir together 1 teaspoon sugar, soy sauce, sesame oil, oyster sauce, ¼ teaspoon salt, and pepper.

• Add bok choy, radishes, and sesame sauce mixture to cooled cooked vegetables, stirring until combined. Cover and refrigerate while preparing bun dough.

• In a small bowl, stir together ¾ cup warm water, yeast, and remaining 2 tablespoons sugar. Let stand until mixture is foamy, approximately 5 minutes. In the bowl of a stand mixer fitted with the dough hook attachment, beat together flour, yeast mixture, and remaining 1 teaspoon salt at low speed until smooth, 6 to 7 minutes. Cover bowl with plastic wrap, and let dough rise at room temperature for 1 hour.

• On a lightly floured surface, knead dough until smooth, 3 to 4 minutes.

• Divide dough into 20 equal portions. Using a rolling pin, roll each portion into a 4-inch circle, making sure edges are extremely thin. Place 1 tablespoon vegetable mixture on each dough circle. Gather edges of dough to encase filling, pinching together to seal buns. Place each bun on a small square piece of parchment paper. While working, cover buns with a damp towel.

• In a bamboo steamer, place buns with parchment paper squares ½ inch apart. (If steamer is small, it may be necessary to cook buns in batches.) Cover steamer with lid.

• In a wok, add cold water to depth of approximately 2 inches, and place steamer on wok. (Water should not touch steamer.) Let stand for 20 minutes.

• Place wok with steamer on stove, and heat over high heat until boiling. Steam for 10 minutes. Turn off heat, and let buns stand for 5 minutes before removing lid. Remove buns. (If cooking buns in batches, fill wok with cold water again, and place remaining buns with parchment inside steamer. Turn heat on high, and repeat cooking process.) Serve warm or at room temperature.

HOW TO MAKE
POT STICKERS

on page 127

Pork Pot Stickers

Makes 36

1 tablespoon minced fresh ginger
1½ tablespoons water, plus more for cooking
½ pound ground pork
1 large egg yolk
4 green onions, diced
1 tablespoon soy sauce
½ tablespoon minced fresh garlic
½ teaspoon ground black pepper
½ teaspoon salt
2 teaspoons vegetable oil, plus more for cooking
36 round pot sticker/dumpling wrappers
Chili-Garlic Sauce (recipe follows)

• In a small bowl, soak minced ginger in 1½ tablespoons water for 5 minutes.
• In a large bowl, combine ground pork and egg yolk. Add ginger water, green onion, soy sauce, garlic, pepper, and salt, stirring until a paste forms. Add 2 teaspoons oil, stirring until combined. Cover and refrigerate overnight.
• With a wrapper in your palm, place 1 rounded teaspoon pork filling in center. Moisten edges of wrapper with water. Fold wrapper in half, pinching together at middle. Pleat edge in a decorative fashion, if desired. (Make sure edges are completely sealed. Keep wrappers covered with a damp towel to keep from drying out.)
• Heat a large skillet over medium heat. Add 2 teaspoons oil to hot pan. Working in batches, add pot stickers, leaving space between them. Fry until lightly browned, approximately 2 minutes. Add ¼ cup water, and cover quickly with lid, agitating pan to keep potstickers from sticking. Cook for 2 minutes. Uncover and cook until water has evaporated and bottoms are nicely browned, approximately 2 minutes. Repeat this step until all dumplings are cooked. Serve hot with Chili-Garlic Sauce.

Chili-Garlic Sauce

Makes 1 cup

½ cup soy sauce
½ cup rice wine vinegar
1 tablespoon firmly packed light brown sugar
2 small cloves garlic
½ teaspoon kosher salt
1 teaspoon sesame oil
⅛ teaspoon dried crushed red pepper

• In a small bowl, stir together soy sauce, vinegar, and brown sugar.
• Using a sharp knife, mince garlic. Sprinkle garlic with salt. Using flat side of knife, press and drag knife over garlic and salt until a paste forms.

• In a medium skillet, heat sesame oil over medium-low heat. Add garlic paste; cook, stirring constantly, until aromatic, approximately 30 seconds. Add soy sauce mixture; cook until sugar dissolves, approximately 30 seconds. Remove from heat. Add crushed red pepper, stirring until combined. Cover and refrigerate until ready to use.

Sesame Balls

Makes 20 *(photo on page 31)*

3 cups glutinous rice flour
¾ cup firmly packed dark brown sugar
2 cups cool water, divided
½ cup Chinese peanut butter*
¼ cup white sesame seeds
¼ cup black sesame seeds
Vegetable oil, for frying

• In a large heatproof bowl, place rice flour, making a well in center of flour.
• In a small saucepan, bring brown sugar and 1 cup water to a boil over medium-high heat. Add sugar mixture to rice flour, stirring with a wooden spoon until a sticky, caramel-brown dough forms.
• Divide dough into 20 equal portions, and roll into balls. To prevent dough from drying out, cover with a damp towel.
• Using a levered 1-teaspoon scoop, divide peanut butter into 20 portions, and roll into balls.
• Press a thumb into center of a dough ball to create a well. Place a peanut butter ball into well, press dough together to cover peanut butter, sealing well, and reshape dough ball. Repeat with remaining peanut butter balls and dough balls.
• Line a rimmed baking sheet with paper towels.
• In a small bowl, stir together sesame seeds until combined.
• In another small bowl, place remaining 1 cup cool water.
• Dip each dough ball in cool water, and roll in sesame seeds. Place sesame balls on prepared baking sheet.
• In a wok, pour oil to a depth of 3 inches, and heat over medium heat until a deep-fry thermometer registers 350°. Fry sesame dough balls, a few at a time, for 2 minutes. Using the back of a spoon, gently apply pressure, and roll balls against side of wok until golden brown. Let drain on prepared baking sheet. Serve warm.

Chinese peanut butter is made with peanuts, soybean oil, sesame, sugar, and salt. Compared to American-style peanut butter, its consistency is thicker and its flavor is significantly less sweet and varies slightly because of the sesame. If a sweeter filling is desired, add 1 tablespoon sugar to the Chinese peanut butter before portioning and rolling it.

Red Bean Paste Cookies
Makes 16

¼ cup plus 2 tablespoons unsalted butter, softened
1 large egg
1 teaspoon vanilla extract
¾ cup plus 1 tablespoon all-purpose flour
¼ cup confectioners' sugar
3½ tablespoons cornstarch
¼ teaspoon salt
¼ cup red bean paste
Garnish: sesame seeds

• In the bowl of a stand mixer fitted with the paddle attachment, beat butter at medium speed until light and creamy.
• In a small bowl, whisk egg. Add 1½ tablespoons whisked egg to butter, and beat until well combined. Add vanilla extract, beating well.
• In a medium bowl, sift together flour, confectioners' sugar, cornstarch, and salt. With mixer at low speed, gradually add flour mixture to butter mixture, beating until combined. Shape dough into a disk, and wrap in plastic wrap. Refrigerate for at least 1 hour.
• Preheat oven to 350°. Line a rimmed baking sheet with parchment paper.
• Turn out dough onto a lightly floured surface, and shape into a 10-inch log. Using a rolling pin, roll out dough into a 12x6-inch rectangle. Spread an even layer of red bean paste onto dough. Starting with a long side, roll up dough jelly-roll style, and pinch seam to seal. Place roll seam side down.
• Using a bench scraper, cut roll, into 16 equal pieces (cookies). Place cookies upright (seam side down) on prepared baking sheet. Brush top of cookies with remaining 2½ tablespoons whisked egg.
• Garnish with a sprinkle of sesame seeds, if desired. Bake cookies until golden, approximately 20 minutes. Serve warm or at room temperature.

Pineapple Cookies
Makes 18

½ cup unsalted butter, softened
2 tablespoons confectioners' sugar
3 tablespoons sweetened condensed milk
1 large egg yolk
⅔ cup all-purpose flour
⅔ cup cake flour
1 tablespoon cornstarch
¼ teaspoon kosher salt
Pineapple Jam (recipe follows)

• In the bowl of a stand mixer fitted with the paddle attachment, beat together butter and confectioners' sugar at medium speed until creamy, 3 to 4 minutes. Add condensed milk and egg yolk, beating until well combined.
• In a medium bowl, whisk together flours, cornstarch, and salt. With mixer at low speed, gradually add flour mixture to butter mixture, beating until combined.
• Shape dough into a disk, and wrap in plastic wrap. Refrigerate for at least 30 minutes.
• Preheat oven to 350°. Line a rimmed baking sheet with parchment paper.
• Turn out dough onto a lightly floured surface. Using a rolling pin, rough out dough to a ⅜-inch thickness. Using a 2-inch flower-shaped cookie cutter, cut 18 cookies, rerolling scraps as necessary. Place cookies 2 inches apart on prepared baking sheet. Using a small wooden pick, etch 3 lines on each petal of cookies, if desired.
• Using a levered 1-teaspoon scoop, divide Pineapple Jam into 18 teaspoon portions. Using your palms, roll Pineapple Jam portions into balls. Place a jam ball in center of each cookie.
• Bake until cookies are golden, approximately 20 minutes.

Pineapple Jam
Makes 2 cups

1 fresh pineapple, cored, finely minced, and drained
¼ teaspoon whole cloves
¼ cup granulated sugar
¼ cup firmly packed light brown sugar
1½ teaspoons fresh lemon juice
⅛ teaspoon salt

• In a large skillet, combine pineapple and cloves. Cook over medium heat, stirring constantly, until most of liquid has evaporated. Add sugars, lemon juice, and salt, stirring to combine. Reduce heat to medium-low; cook, stirring constantly, until pineapple is transparent and jam is golden, 30 to 40 minutes. Remove from heat. Discard cloves. Let jam cool completely before using.

SESAME BALLS
recipe on page 29

France

When tea arrived in France in the early part of the 17th century, it was a luxury beverage that only the highest social classes could afford. Nowadays, tea is enjoyed throughout France, from the bucolic countrysides to the bustling cities. *Salons de thé* offer marvelous options for afternoon tea, a practice popularized here in the mid-1800s, which naturally includes delicious pâtiserries and sweets unique to French cuisine. The country has also been home to many well-known porcelain manufacturers, such as Bernardaud, which have been producing stunningly beautiful, yet practical, tea sets and accoutrements for centuries.

In the French style, gold-trimmed china and adornments bring joie de vivre to this modern-day afternoon tea. A Francophile's dream, each course of this inspired menu highlights several of the country's delectable *bonnes bouches*. Serve guests teatime variations of French classics, such as duck à l'orange in flaky croissants, a tea lover's version of the ever-elegant opera cake, and delicate macarons with a rich crème fraîche filling, along with delicious teas all perfectly paired for each course.

The
MENU

SCONE
Apricot-Lavender Scones
🍵 *Paris Garden Tea*

SAVORIES
Lemon-Dill Salmon
Mousse Canapés
Olive-Comté Gougères
Duck à l'Orange Croissants
🍵 *Parisian Tango Tea*

SWEETS
Petits Lemon-Pistachio Éclairs
French Opera Tea Cakes
Strawberry Macarons with
Crème Fraîche Filling
🍵 *Marie Antoinette Tea*

*Tea Pairings by Paris In A Cup,
714-538-9411, parisinacup.com*

RECOMMENDED
CONDIMENT

• Clotted Cream

Apricot-Lavender Scones
Makes 9

2½ cups all-purpose flour
⅓ cup granulated sugar
1 tablespoon baking powder
½ teaspoon salt
¼ cup cold unsalted butter
⅓ cup chopped dried apricots
1½ teaspoons dried culinary lavender
½ cup plus 2 tablespoons cold heavy
   whipping cream, divided
½ teaspoon vanilla extract
1 large egg

• Preheat oven to 375º. Line a rimmed baking sheet with parchment paper.
• In a large bowl, whisk together flour, sugar, baking powder, and salt. Using a pastry blender or 2 forks, cut in cold butter until it resembles coarse crumbs. Add apricots and lavender, stirring well.
• In a small bowl, whisk together ½ cup plus 1 tablespoon cold cream, vanilla extract, and egg. Add cream mixture to flour mixture, stirring until mixture is evenly moist. (If dough seems dry, add more cream, 1 tablespoon at a time.) Working gently, bring mixture together with hands until a dough forms.
• Turn out dough onto a lightly floured surface, and knead gently 4 to 5 times. Using a rolling pin, roll out dough to a 1-inch thickness. Using a 2¼-inch fluted round cutter, cut 9 scones from dough, rerolling scraps as necessary. Place scones 2 inches apart on prepared baking sheet. Brush tops of scones with remaining 1 tablespoon cold cream.
• Bake until edges of scones are golden brown and a wooden pick inserted in centers comes out clean, approximately 18 minutes.

Lemon-Dill Salmon Mousse Canapés
Makes 12   (*photo on page 38*)

1½ tablespoons warm water
½ teaspoon unflavored gelatin
1 (4-ounce) package thinly sliced smoked salmon
½ cup sour cream
1 tablespoon finely snipped fresh dill
1 teaspoon fresh lemon zest
1 teaspoon fresh lemon juice
1 teaspoon heavy whipping cream
⅛ teaspoon salt
6 very thin slices whole wheat bread
Garnish: fresh dill sprigs

• In a small bowl, stir together 1½ tablespoons warm water and gelatin. Let cool.
• In the work bowl of a food processor, pulse together cooled gelatin mixture, smoked salmon, sour cream, dill, lemon zest, lemon juice, whipping cream, and salt until combined. Transfer salmon mousse to a covered container, and refrigerate until cold and firm, approximately 6 hours.
• Preheat oven to 350º. Line a rimmed baking sheet with parchment paper.
• Using a serrated bread knife, trim and discard crusts from bread slices. Cut each bread slice into 2 (2½x1-inch) rectangles. Place bread rectangles 2 inches apart on prepared baking sheet.
• Bake until bread rectangles are firm and crisp, 7 to 10 minutes. Let cool completely.
• Just before serving, place chilled salmon mousse in a piping bag fitted with a large open-star tip (Wilton #1M). Pipe mousse in a scrolled pattern onto each toasted bread rectangle.
• Garnish with dill, if desired. Serve immediately.

Olive-Comté Gougères
Makes 30   (*photo on page 38*)

½ cup water
½ cup whole milk
½ cup unsalted butter
¼ teaspoon salt
¼ teaspoon ground black pepper
1 cup all-purpose flour
4 large eggs
¾ cup Comté cheese
¼ cup finely grated Parmesan cheese
2 tablespoons finely minced Niçoise olives

• Preheat oven to 400º. Line 2 rimmed baking sheets with parchment paper.
• In a medium saucepan, bring ½ cup water, milk, butter, salt, and pepper to a boil over medium-high heat. Reduce heat to low; add flour. Using a wooden spoon, stir mixture until a smooth dough forms, approximately 2 minutes.
• Transfer dough to a large bowl. Let cool for 1 minute. With a mixer at medium speed, add eggs, one at a time, beating until well incorporated. Add Comté and Parmesan cheeses, beating until incorporated. With mixer at low speed, add olives, beating until combined.
• Transfer dough to a piping bag fitted with a large open-star tip (Wilton #1M). Pipe 30 (1¼-inch) rosettes of dough 2 inches apart onto prepared baking sheets.
• Bake gougères until puffed and golden brown, 20 to 22 minutes. Serve warm.

LEMON-DILL SALMON MOUSSE CANAPÉS
and OLIVE-COMTÉ GOUGÈRES
recipes on page 37

Duck à l'Orange Croissants

Makes 12

3 skin-on duck breasts
1 teaspoon ground coriander seed
½ teaspoon ground fennel seed
½ teaspoon salt
⅛ teaspoon ground black pepper
⅛ teaspoon ground red pepper
2 teaspoons olive oil
Orange Glaze (recipe follows)
12 small croissants
Lemon-Pepper Aïoli (recipe follows)
2 cups spring mix lettuce
24 orange sections

• Preheat oven to 350°. Line a rimmed baking sheet with foil.
• Using a sharp knife, deeply score skin of duck breasts in a cross-hatch pattern.

• In a small bowl, stir together coriander seed, fennel seed, salt, black pepper, and red pepper.
• Season duck with spice mixture, using most of mixture on underside of duck, and using remainder on skin.
• In a sauté pan, heat oil over medium-high heat. Place duck breasts in pan, fat side down. Sear duck breasts until nicely browned, 3 to 5 minutes per side. (Reduce heat to medium, if necessary.) Reserve 1 tablespoon fat from pan for Orange Glaze.
• Place duck breasts, skin side up, on prepared baking sheet.
• Bake, brushing frequently with Orange Glaze, until a meat thermometer inserted in thickest portion of duck registers 135° to 170°, approximately 10 minutes, depending on desired degree of doneness. Let duck rest for 15 minutes.
• Using a sharp knife, thinly slice duck.
• Using a serrated bread knife, cut croissants in half horizontally. Spread a thin layer of Lemon-Pepper Aïoli onto cut sides of each croissant. Place a layer of lettuce, 2 orange sections, and 2 duck slices on top of bottom half of a croissant. Cover with top half of croissant, aïoli side down. Repeat with remaining ingredients. Serve immediately.

Orange Glaze
Makes approximately ¾ cup

1 tablespoon reserved duck fat
1 tablespoon minced shallots
½ cup chicken broth
1 tablespoon orange zest
½ cup fresh orange juice
¼ cup firmly packed light brown sugar
1 tablespoon stone-ground mustard
1 tablespoon sherry vinegar
⅛ teaspoon salt
⅛ teaspoon ground black pepper

• In a medium sauté pan, heat duck fat over medium-high heat. Add shallots; reduce heat to low. Cook until shallots are tender, 2 to 3 minutes. Add broth and all remaining ingredients, stirring to combine. Increase heat to medium-high; cook, stirring frequently, until mixture is thick and syrupy, 10 to 12 minutes. Use immediately.

Lemon-Pepper Aïoli
Makes ⅓ cup

⅓ cup mayonnaise
½ teaspoon fresh lemon zest
⅛ teaspoon ground black pepper

• In a small bowl, stir together mayonnaise, lemon zest, and pepper. Use immediately, or refrigerate until needed.

Petits Lemon-Pistachio Éclairs
Makes 48

¾ cup water
¼ cup plus 2 tablespoons unsalted butter,
  softened and cubed
2 teaspoons granulated sugar
¼ teaspoon salt
¾ cup all-purpose flour
3 large eggs, at room temperature
Lemon Whipped Cream (recipe follows)
Creamy Glaze (recipe follows)
Garnish: chopped roasted salted pistachios

• Preheat oven to 400º. Line 2 rimmed baking sheets with parchment paper or silicone baking mats.
• In a medium saucepan, combine ¾ cup water, butter, sugar, and salt. Cook over medium heat until butter melts. Add flour, stirring vigorously with a wooden spoon. Cook and stir until dough pulls away from sides of pan, 1 to 2 minutes. Remove from heat, and let stand for 2 minutes, stirring a few times to cool dough.
• Transfer dough to a large bowl. With a mixer at medium speed, add eggs, one at a time, beating until well incorporated. (Dough should be smooth and shiny.)
• Transfer dough to a piping bag fitted with a medium round tip (Wilton #12). Pipe 2½-inch lengths of dough onto prepared baking sheets. (Pat dough with damp finger if it needs additional shaping.)
• Bake for 15 minutes. Reduce oven temperature to 350º. Bake until éclairs are very golden brown, approximately 10 minutes more. (Insides will be dry.) Let cool completely.
• Using a sharp knife, make small slits in 2 places on bottom of each eclair.
• Place Lemon Whipped Cream in a piping bag fitted with a small open-star tip (Wilton #18). Pipe cream into éclairs through bottom slits.
• Dip tops of éclairs into Creamy Glaze, letting excess drip off. Place éclairs glaze side up on a wire rack.
• Garnish glaze with pistachios, if desired.
• Serve immediately, or place in a covered container, and refrigerate for up to 2 hours.

• In a deep bowl, beat together cold cream, confectioners' sugar, and vanilla extract with a mixer at high speed until soft peaks form. Add lemon curd, beating just until incorporated. Use immediately, or cover and refrigerate for up to 2 hours.

Lemon Whipped Cream
Makes 2 cups

1 cup cold heavy whipping cream
2 tablespoons confectioners' sugar
½ teaspoon vanilla extract
⅓ cup lemon curd

Creamy Glaze
Makes 2 cups

2 cups confectioners' sugar
¼ cup whole milk

• In a medium bowl, whisk together confectioners' sugar and milk until combined and smooth. (If needed, adjust thickness of glaze by adding more milk to make thinner, or more confectioners' sugar to thicken.) Use immediately.

French Opera Tea Cakes

Makes 20

6 large egg whites, at room temperature
2 tablespoons granulated sugar
2¼ cups confectioners' sugar
2 cups almond meal
2 tablespoons loose black tea leaves*, ground
¼ cup teaspoon salt
6 large eggs
½ teaspoon vanilla extract
½ cup all-purpose flour
3 tablespoons unsalted butter, melted and cooled
Paris Tea Syrup (recipe follows)
Vanilla Buttercream (recipe follows)
Dark Chocolate Ganache (recipe follows)
Semisweet Chocolate Ganache (recipe follows)
Garnish: gold leaf

• Preheat oven to 425°. Lightly spray 3 (13x9-inch) baking pans with baking spray with flour. Line pans with parchment paper, and spray again.
• In a large bowl, beat egg whites with a mixer at high speed until frothy. Gradually add granulated sugar, beating until glossy stiff peaks form, approximately 3 minutes.
• In another large bowl, whisk together confectioners' sugar, almond meal, ground tea, and salt. Add eggs and vanilla extract, and beat together with a mixer at high speed for 3 minutes. Gently fold in flour.
• Gently stir one-fourth of almond meal mixture into beaten egg whites. Fold remaining almond meal mixture and melted butter into eggs whites. Divide batter among prepared baking pans. Using an offset spatula, level surface of batter.
• Bake until surface of cakes spring back when lightly touched in centers, 5 to 7 minutes. Let cool completely in pans.
• Line a rimmed baking pan with parchment paper.
• Place one cake layer, top side up, onto prepared baking pan. Brush top of cake with a thin layer of Paris Tea Syrup.
• Using an offset spatula, spread half of Vanilla Buttercream onto cake, creating a level surface. Using an offset spatula, spread half of Dark Chocolate Ganache over buttercream layer, creating a level surface. Place another cake layer on top of ganache. Brush top of cake with a thin layer of Paris Tea Syrup. Using an offset spatula, spread remaining Vanilla Buttercream onto cake, creating a level surface. Using an offset spatula, spread remaining Dark Chocolate Ganache over buttercream layer, creating a level surface. Top with remaining cake layer. Brush top of cake with a thin layer of Paris Tea Syrup. Using an offset spatula, spread Semisweet Chocolate Ganache over top cake layer, creating a smooth, level surface.

• Place wooden picks at each corner of stacked cake to secure layers. Refrigerate cake overnight.
• Using a long, sharp knife, trim and discard 1 inch from cake edges. Cut cake into 20 (2½x1¼-inch) rectangles.
• Garnish each rectangle with gold leaf, if desired.

Paris Tea Syrup

Makes approximately ½ cup

½ cup water
½ cup granulated sugar
2 tea bags Harney & Sons' Paris black tea

• In a small saucepan, bring ½ cup water and sugar to a boil over medium-high heat, stirring occasionally, until sugar dissolves. Remove from heat. Add tea bags; steep for 5 minutes. Discard tea bags. Let syrup cool before using.

Vanilla Buttercream

Makes 4 cups

1 cup unsalted butter, softened
4 cups confectioners' sugar
¼ cup plus 1 tablespoon heavy whipping cream
½ teaspoon vanilla extract
⅛ teaspoon salt

• In a large bowl, beat together butter, confectioners' sugar, cream, vanilla extract, and salt with a mixer at high speed until light and fluffy. Use immediately.

Dark Chocolate Ganache

Makes 1 cup

½ cup whole milk
½ cup heavy whipping cream
2 (4-ounce) bars bittersweet chocolate, finely chopped
4 tablespoons unsalted butter, softened

• In a medium saucepan, heat milk and cream until very hot and steaming. Remove from heat. Add chocolate, stirring until chocolate melts and mixture is smooth. Add butter, 1 tablespoon at a time, stirring well after each addition. Let cool slightly before using.

Semisweet Chocolate Ganache

Makes ⅔ cup

⅔ cup heavy whipping cream
1 (4-ounce) bar semisweet chocolate, finely chopped

• In a small saucepan, heat cream until very hot and steaming. Remove from heat. Add chocolate, stirring until chocolate melts and mixture is smooth. Let cool slightly before using.

*We used Harney &
Sons' Paris black tea
blend, harney.com.

Strawberry Macarons with Crème Fraîche Filling

Makes 20

3 large egg whites
2 cups confectioners' sugar
1 cup sifted almond meal
⅛ teaspoon salt
1 tablespoon granulated sugar
1 teaspoon strawberry extract
Pink paste food coloring
Crème Fraîche Filling (recipe follows)

• Place egg whites in a large bowl, and let stand at room temperature for exactly 3 hours. (Aging egg whites in this manner is essential to creating the perfect macaron.)
• Line 2 rimmed baking sheets with parchment paper. Using a pencil, draw 40 (1¼-inch) circles 2 inches apart onto parchment; turn parchment over.
• In the work bowl of a food processor, pulse together confectioners' sugar, almond meal, and salt until combined.
• In the bowl of a stand mixer fitted with the whisk attachment, beat egg whites at medium-high speed until frothy. With mixer at high speed, gradually add granulated sugar and strawberry extract, beating until thick, shiny, and creamy, approximately 5 minutes. Add food coloring to achieve desired color. Using a large spatula, fold in almond meal mixture until batter falls in thick ribbons. Let stand for 15 minutes.
• Transfer batter to a piping bag fitted with a medium round tip (Wilton #12). Pipe batter into drawn circles on prepared baking sheets. Tap baking sheets vigorously on counter 5 to 7 times to release air bubbles. Let stand at room temperature for 1 hour before baking to help develop the macaron's signature crisp exterior when baked. (Macarons should feel dry to the touch and should not stick to finger.)
• Preheat oven to 275°.
• Bake until macarons are firm to the touch, approximately 20 minutes. Let cool completely on pans. Transfer macarons to an airtight container with layers separated by wax paper. Refrigerate until ready to fill and serve.
• Place Crème Fraîche Filling in a piping bag fitted with a medium round tip (Wilton #12). Pipe filling onto flat side of 20 macarons. Top each with a remaining macaron, flat side down. Push down lightly and twist so filling spreads to edges. Serve immediately.

MAKE-AHEAD TIP: Wrap unfilled macarons in plastic wrap in groups of 4 to 6 to prevent crushing or breaking, and place in airtight containers. Refrigerate for up to 2 days until needed. Let come to room temperature before filling and serving.

Crème Fraîche Filling

Makes 1½ cups

½ cup cold heavy whipping cream
3 tablespoons confectioners' sugar
½ teaspoon vanilla extract
½ cup crème fraîche

• In a small deep bowl, beat together whipping cream, confectioners' sugar, and vanilla extract with a mixer at high speed until thickened. Add crème fraîche, beating just until incorporated. Use immediately.

India

As one of the largest producers of tea in the world, it is only natural for India to have a unique tea culture. The regions of Assam, Darjeeling, and the Nilgiris are internationally recognized for the distinctive flavors of their teas. The nation is also known for the traditional Masala chai beverage, which is a robust black tea, such as one from Assam, mixed with cardamom, ginger, cloves, peppercorn, and cinnamon and steeped in hot milk. Although *chai* is the Hindi word for tea, the term has become synonymous in the Western world with the sweet, spicy drink.

Accompanied with various Indian teas, the festive fare of this afternoon tea, which celebrates India's diverse and flavorful cuisine, includes savory offerings like lentil samosas and sweet options like *ladoo*. Scones laced with pistachios and dried rose petals can be served as a first course, or in typical British style, as a second. Marvel guests with the different flavors incorporated throughout the menu, and astonish them with a table set in the vibrant and colorful styles often utilized in Indian culture.

"Good tea is like an Indian movie breaking out into a mass choreographed dance of taste in your mouth."

—Bianca Shah,
International Tea Importers

The MENU

SCONE
Rose Petal–Pistachio Scones
*Darjeeling Risheehat Estate
Organic FTGFOP-1*

SAVORIES
Shrimp Salad Cups
Curried Cucumber Tea Sandwiches
Lentil Samosas
Craigmore Estate FOP

SWEETS
Coconut Ladoo
Nankha Tai Cookies
Date, Coconut, Ginger
& Chocolate Tarts
*Mangalam Estate
Golden Tip Assam*

*Tea Pairings by Chado Tea,
562-801-9600, chadotea.com*

RECOMMENDED
CONDIMENTS

• Clotted Cream
• Orange Marmalade

Rose Petal–Pistachio Scones
Makes 12

3 cups all-purpose flour
¼ cup granulated sugar
2 teaspoons baking powder
½ teaspoon kosher salt
½ cup cold unsalted butter, cubed
3 tablespoons food-grade dried rose petals
¼ cup finely ground salted pistachios
1 large egg, lightly beaten

1¼ cups plus 1 tablespoon heavy whipping cream, divided
2 tablespoons confectioners' sugar
Garnish: food-grade dried rose petals, finely chopped pistachios

• Preheat oven to 375°. Line a rimmed baking sheet with parchment paper.
• In a large bowl, whisk together flour, granulated sugar, baking powder, and salt. Using a pastry blender or 2 forks, cut in cold butter until mixture resembles coarse

crumbs. Add rose petals and pistachios, stirring until combined. Make a well in center of flour mixture. Add egg and 1¼ cups cream, stirring with a fork until a dough forms. Gently knead in bowl until dough comes together.

• Turn out dough onto a lightly floured surface. Using a rolling pin, roll out dough to a 1-inch thickness. Using a 1½-inch round cutter, cut 12 scones from dough, rerolling scraps as necessary. Place scones 2 inches apart on prepared baking sheet.

• Bake scones until edges are golden brown and a wooden pick inserted in centers comes out clean, 15 to 30 minutes.

• In a small bowl, whisk together confectioners' sugar and remaining 1 tablespoon cream until smooth. Brush top of scones with sugar mixture. While sugar mixture is still wet, garnish with rose petals and pistachios, if desired.

Shrimp Salad Cups
Makes 18

1 cup all-purpose flour
½ cup semolina
1 tablespoon cumin seeds, roasted
1¼ teaspoons ground green cardamom, divided
1 teaspoon chili powder
1 teaspoon kosher salt
¾ cup yogurt
2 tablespoons butter, softened
¼ cup minced green apple
¼ cup minced fresh pineapple
2 tablespoons chopped fresh cilantro
2 teaspoons olive oil
18 small cooked shrimp

• In a large bowl, stir together flour, semolina, cumin seeds, 1 teaspoon cardamom, chili powder, and salt until combined. Add yogurt and butter, stirring well. Knead until a soft dough forms. Cover dough with plastic wrap, and refrigerate for 30 minutes.

• Preheat oven to 375°. Lightly grease 18 wells of a 24-well mini muffin pan.

• Using a rolling pin, roll out dough on a lightly floured surface to an ⅛-inch thickness. Using a 2¼-inch square cutter, cut 18 squares from dough. Place dough squares in prepared wells of muffin pan.

• Bake until squares (shells) are browned and crisp, approximately 15 minutes. Let cool in pan for 10 minutes before removing to wire racks to let cool completely.

• In a medium bowl, gently toss together apple, pineapple, cilantro, oil, and remaining ¼ teaspoon cardamom. Spoon fruit mixture into prepared shells. Top each filled shell with a shrimp. Serve immediately.

Curried Cucumber Tea Sandwiches
Makes 8

½ English cucumber, peeled and sliced ⅛-inch thick
⅛ teaspoon salt
4 ounces cream cheese, softened
2 tablespoons sliced almonds, toasted
2 tablespoons mango chutney
2 teaspoons curry powder
8 thin slices white sandwich bread

• Lightly sprinkle cucumber slices with salt.

• In a small bowl, stir together cream cheese, almonds, chutney, and curry powder until combined. Spread 1 tablespoon cream cheese mixture in an even layer onto each bread slice. Arrange cucumber slices atop cream cheese side of 4 bread slices. Cover with remaining 4 bread slices, cream cheese side down.

• Using a serrated bread knife, trim and discard crusts from sandwiches. Cut each sandwich into 2 rectangles. Serve immediately, or cover with damp paper towels, place in a covered container, and refrigerate until serving time.

HOW TO MAKE
LENTIL SAMOSAS
_____

on page 129

- In a small skillet, heat 1 teaspoon oil until hot. Add cumin seeds, and let sizzle. Add jalapeño, onion, and ½ teaspoon salt; sauté over medium heat for 2 to 3 minutes. Add lentils, mango chutney, turmeric, garam masala, coriander, and lime zest, stirring until vegetables are coated with spices.
- In a medium bowl, whisk together 1½ cups flour, curry powder, remaining 1 tablespoon oil, and remaining 1 teaspoon salt. Using hands, mix dough so oil is evenly distributed in dough. Add ½ cup water, ¼ cup at a time, kneading until dough is soft. Cover with plastic wrap to keep from drying out. Let dough rest for 20 to 30 minutes.
- In a small bowl, whisk together remaining 1 tablespoon flour and remaining 2 tablespoons water until combined.
- Divide dough into 10 equal portions.
- Rub oil onto a clean work surface. Working with one portion of dough at a time, using a rolling pin, roll out dough into a thin (6- to 7-inch diameter) circle on oiled surface. Using a sharp knife, cut circle in half to create 2 semicircles. Working with one semicircle at a time and keeping rounded edge toward you, fold left corner toward center, and brush flour paste on folded left side. Fold right side over left to form a triangle, and press gently until sides stick.
- Open dough triangle gently to form a cone, and fill with lentil mixture, being careful not to overfill. Spread flour paste onto top edges of cone. Using a fork, seal top edges of cone, enclosing filling. Repeat with remaining dough and lentil mixture.
- Fill a large stockpot halfway with oil, and heat over medium heat until a deep-fry thermometer registers 350°. Drop samosas into hot oil, 4 at a time. Fry on both sides until golden brown, 2 to 3 minutes.
- Serve with Cilantro-Mint Chutney, if desired.

Lentil Samosas
Makes 20

1 teaspoon plus 1 tablespoon vegetable oil, divided, plus more for work surface and frying
½ teaspoon cumin seeds
1 small jalapeño, finely chopped
2 tablespoons finely chopped red onion
1½ teaspoons kosher salt, divided
½ cup cooked green lentils
3 tablespoons mango chutney
½ teaspoon turmeric powder
½ teaspoon garam masala
½ teaspoon ground coriander
½ teaspoon fresh lime zest
1½ cups plus 1 tablespoon all-purpose flour, divided
½ teaspoon curry powder
½ plus cup 2 tablespoons chilled water, divided
Cilantro-Mint Chutney (recipe follows)

Cilantro-Mint Chutney
Makes 1 cup

1 cup packed fresh cilantro sprigs
½ cup packed fresh mint leaves
3 tablespoons chopped red onion
2 tablespoons water
1 tablespoon fresh lime juice
1 teaspoon chopped fresh small green chiles, such as serrano or Thai
1 teaspoon granulated sugar
¾ teaspoon salt
¼ cup thick, full-fat Greek yogurt

- In the container of a blender, process together cilantro, mint, onion, 2 tablespoons water, lime juice, chiles, sugar, and salt until combined. Add yogurt, stirring until combined. Serve immediately.

COCONUT LADOO
recipe on page 55

NANKHA
TAI COOKIES
recipe on page 55

Coconut Ladoo

Makes 18 *(photo on page 53)*

2 cups desiccated coconut, plus more for rolling
1 cup whole milk
¾ cup granulated sugar
¼ cup chickpea flour (gram flour)
¼ teaspoon ground cardamom
1 cup broken salted cashews

• In a small bowl, stir together desiccated coconut and milk. Refrigerate for 2 hours.
• In a medium skillet, heat together coconut mixture, sugar, chickpea flour, and cardamom over medium heat until mixture thickens. Remove from heat. Add cashews, stirring well. Let cool for 10 minutes.
• Using a levered 1-tablespoon scoop, divide coconut mixture into 18 portions. Roll each portion into a ball. (If coconut mixture is too warm, it will be difficult to roll.) Roll balls in more desiccated coconut. Store in an airtight container in the refrigerator for up to a week. Serve cold or at room temperature.

Nankha Tai Cookies

Makes 12 *(photo on page 53)*

½ cup granulated sugar
½ cup ghee (clarified butter), at room temperature
1 tablespoon full-fat Greek yogurt
2 cups almond flour
½ cup chickpea flour (gram flour)
1 teaspoon baking powder
½ teaspoon baking soda
½ teaspoon ground cardamom
⅛ teaspoon ground nutmeg
12 blanched whole almonds

• In the work bowl of a food processor, pulse sugar to a fine powder. Add ghee and yogurt, pulsing until mixture is creamy and fluffy. Add flours, baking powder, baking soda, cardamom, and nutmeg, pulsing until blended. (Dough will resemble coarse crumbs.) Shape dough onto a disk, and wrap in plastic wrap. Refrigerate for 30 minutes.
• Preheat oven to 350°. Line a rimmed baking sheet with parchment paper.
• Using a rolling pin, gently roll out dough on a lightly floured surface. Using a 1½-inch round cutter, cut 12 cookies from dough, rerolling scraps as necessary. Place cookies 2 inches apart on prepared baking sheet. (Dough will be fragile.) Place an almond in center of each cookie.
• Bake until cookies are lightly browned, approximately 12 minutes. Let cool on baking sheet for 5 minutes before removing to a wire rack to let cool completely.

Date, Coconut, Ginger & Chocolate Tarts

Makes 15

¾ cup pitted Medjool dates, divided
5 ounces 70% dark chocolate,* divided
1 cup whole raw almonds
2 tablespoons coconut oil, melted and divided
¼ teaspoon plus ⅛ teaspoon salt, divided
1 cup coconut cream
1 tablespoon finely chopped crystalized ginger
½ teaspoon vanilla extract
Garnish: sweetened whipped cream, grated chocolate,
    fresh raspberries, fresh mint sprigs

• Lightly grease 15 (2-ounce) silicone molds.
• In a medium bowl, cover ½ cup dates with warm water. Let soak for 10 minutes. Drain well, and pat dates dry.
• In a small microwave-safe bowl, heat 2 ounces chocolate on high in 30-second intervals, stirring between each, until melted and smooth (approximately 1½ minutes total).
• In the work bowl of a food processor, pulse together dates and almonds until finely ground. Add melted chocolate, 1 tablespoon coconut oil, and ¼ teaspoon salt, processing until incorporated. Divide date mixture among prepared molds. Place molds on a rimmed baking sheet, and freeze until firm.
• In a medium saucepan, heat together coconut cream, remaining 1 tablespoon coconut oil, and remaining 3 ounces chocolate until chocolate melts.
• In the work bowl of a food processor, process together chocolate mixture, crystallized ginger, vanilla extract, remaining ¼ cup dates, and remaining ⅛ teaspoon salt until smooth. Divide chocolate mixture among frozen date crusts. Freeze for at least 2 hours. Remove from molds. Thaw in the refrigerator for 1 hour before serving.
• Garnish with whipped cream, grated chocolate, raspberries, and mint, if desired.

We used Green & Black's Organic 70% Dark Chocolate.

Japan

Tea bushes were first planted in Japan in the 9th century after Emperor Saga tasted tea Buddhist monks brought with them when they returned from studying in China. For the next seven centuries, however, tea cultivation and drinking was primarily limited to monasteries. Nowadays, Japanese green teas, such as sencha, gyokuro, and genmaicha, are widely available and are best known for their lovely umami flavor notes and bright green color. Matcha, a powdered tea made by grinding tencha green tea, is used in the Japanese tea ceremony, which is strikingly beautiful in its simplicity.

With the elegant, Imperial-style pattern of Royal Crown Derby's "Traditional Imari" decorating the table, this Japanese-inspired afternoon tea incorporates matcha in a delightful almond and black sesame scone, as well as in a simple, crunchy cookie. Traditional dishes like noodle bowls, yakitori, and sushi make for a memorable savories course, while colorful mochi balls studded with mango- and strawberry-flavored ice cream centers, along with pretty petits fours laced with cherry and topped with delicate pink fondant blossoms round out the sweets.

The
MENU

SCONE
Matcha, Almond & Black
Sesame Scones
Gyokuro Japanese Green

SAVORIES
Udon Noodle Bowls
Chicken Yakitori
Sushi Balls with Ginger Miso Sauce
Houjicha Roasted Green Tea

SWEETS
Cherry Blossom Petits Fours
Strawberry & Mango Mochi Balls
Matcha-Lemon Cookies
Bancha Japanese Green

Tea Pairings by Global Tea Mart,
844-208-2337, globalteamart.com

RECOMMENDED
CONDIMENT

• Lemon Curd

Matcha, Almond & Black Sesame Scones
Makes 12

2⅔ cups all-purpose flour, divided
1 cup almond flour
⅓ cup plus 2 tablespoons and 2 teaspoons
   granulated sugar, divided
1 tablespoon plus 1 teaspoon culinary-grade
   matcha powder
1 teaspoon baking powder
1¼ teaspoons kosher salt, divided
¼ cup plus 2 tablespoons cold unsalted butter, cubed
½ cup sliced almonds, toasted and cooled
¾ cup whole milk
1 large egg, lightly beaten
2 tablespoons plus 2 teaspoons firmly packed light
   brown sugar
1½ teaspoons black sesame seeds
¼ cup unsalted butter, melted

• Preheat oven to 400°. Line a rimmed baking sheet
with parchment paper.
• In a large bowl, whisk together 2 cups all-purpose flour,
almond flour, ⅓ cup granulated sugar, matcha powder,
baking powder, and 1 teaspoon salt. Using a pastry blender
or 2 forks, cut in cold butter until it resembles coarse
crumbs. Add sliced almonds, stirring to combine. Add milk,
stirring until mixture is evenly moist. (If mixture seems dry,
add more milk, 1 tablespoon at a time.) Working gently,
bring mixture together with hands until a dough forms.
• Turn out dough onto a lightly floured surface, and
gently knead 4 to 5 times. Using a rolling pin, roll out
dough to a ¾-inch thickness. Using a 2½-inch fluted
round cutter, cut 12 scones from dough, rerolling scraps
as necessary. Place scones 2 inches apart on prepared
baking sheet. Brush tops of scones with egg.
• In a small bowl, whisk together remaining ⅔ cup all-
purpose flour, remaining 2 tablespoons and 2 teaspoons
granulated sugar, brown sugar, sesame seeds, and
remaining ¼ teaspoon salt. Drizzle with melted butter,
and stir with a wooden spoon until combined. Crumble
with fingers until desired consistency is reached, and
sprinkle onto scones.
• Bake until edges of scones are golden brown and
a wooden pick inserted in centers comes out clean,
12 to 15 minutes.

Udon Noodle Bowls
Makes 6 servings

12 cups water
1 (8-ounce) package whole wheat udon noodles
2 tablespoons rice vinegar
3 cups beef broth

3 tablespoons extra-virgin olive oil
1½ cup thinly sliced fresh baby portobello mushrooms
¾ pound medium fresh shrimp, peeled and deveined
1½ cups fresh baby spinach
3 tablespoons minced green onion
1 tablespoon mirin
2 teaspoons minced garlic
1 teaspoon grated fresh ginger
1 teaspoon chopped fresh mint
1 teaspoon chopped fresh cilantro
¼ teaspoon ground white pepper

• In a large stockpot, bring 12 cups water to a boil over
medium-high heat. Add noodles, and reduce heat to low.
Simmer for 5 minutes. Strain noodles, and rinse with
cold water.
• Transfer noodles to a large bowl. Add rice vinegar,
stirring well. Cover with plastic wrap, pressing wrap
directly onto surface of noodles to prevent drying out.
Refrigerate until ready to use, up to a day.
• In a large saucepan, bring broth to a boil over
medium-high heat. Reduce heat to low, and simmer
until ready to serve.
• In a large sauté pan, heat oil over medium heat. Add
mushrooms; cook for 3 minutes. Add shrimp; cook until
one side is pink, approximately 3 minutes. Turn shrimp
over. Add spinach, green onion, mirin, garlic, ginger,
mint, cilantro, and pepper. Cook until shrimp are done,
approximately 4 minutes. Add shrimp mixture to broth.
• Divide noodles among 6 serving bowls. Ladle shrimp
mixture over noodles. Serve immediately.

- In the same sauté pan, add 2 tablespoons vegetable oil. Cook chicken over medium heat until cooked through, approximately 5 minutes per side. Transfer to a heatproof bowl.
- Divide chicken among 24 skewers. Brush all sides of chicken with warm sesame marinade. Serve warm or at room temperature.
- Garnish serving plates with cabbage and green onion, if desired.

Sushi Balls with Ginger Miso Sauce
Makes 12

1 cup water
¼ cup sushi rice
1 teaspoon kosher salt
1 teaspoon rice vinegar
2 baby cucumbers
6 slices tuna sashimi
6 slices salmon sashimi
Garnish: shaved red radish
Ginger-Miso Sauce (recipe follows)

- In a medium saucepan, bring 1 cup water, rice, and salt to a boil over medium-high heat. Reduce heat to low, and simmer for 20 minutes. Add rice vinegar, stirring until combined. Spread rice mixture on a rimmed baking sheet. Let cool completely. Cover with plastic wrap, and refrigerate until ready to use.
- Using a levered 1-tablespoon scoop, divide rice into 12 portions.
- Using a mandoline, cut 36 thin slices from cucumbers. Using a ¾-inch round cutter, cut a round from each cucumber slice, discarding scraps. Arrange 3 cucumber rounds atop each rice portion.
- Using a ¾-inch square cutter, cut 6 squares from tuna and 6 squares from salmon, discarding scraps. Place a fish square on atop cucumber rounds on each rice portion.
- Garnish with radish, if desired.
- Serve cold with Ginger-Miso Sauce.

Ginger-Miso Sauce
Makes ½ cup

¼ cup sushi ginger, minced
1 tablespoon minced garlic
1 tablespoon soy sauce
1 tablespoon mirin
2 teaspoons white miso paste

- In a small bowl, whisk together ginger, garlic, soy sauce, mirin, and miso paste. Use immediately, or cover and refrigerate for up to a day.

Chicken Yakitori
Makes 24

¼ cup firmly packed dark brown sugar
2 tablespoons soy sauce
2 teaspoons minced garlic
½ teaspoon freshly grated ginger root
1 pound boneless skinless chicken thighs, cubed
¼ cup sesame seeds, toasted
2 tablespoons sake
2 teaspoons mirin
2 tablespoons vegetable oil
Garnish: coarsely grated purple cabbage, chopped green onion

- In a medium bowl, whisk together brown sugar, soy sauce, garlic, and ginger. Add chicken, stirring until coated. Cover with plastic wrap, and marinate in refrigerator for at least 1 hour.
- Strain chicken, reserving marinade.
- In a medium sauté pan, whisk marinade over medium heat. Cook until marinade comes to a boil. Reduce heat to low, and simmer until mixture thickens, approximately 3 minutes.
- Transfer mixture to a heatproof bowl. Add sesame seeds, sake, and mirin, stirring until incorporated.

MANGO MOCHI BALL
recipe on page 66

MATCHA-LEMON COOKIES
recipe on page 66

Cherry Blossom Petits Fours

Makes 16

½ cup unsalted butter, softened
1 cup granulated sugar
2 large eggs
¼ teaspoon vanilla bean paste
½ cup plus 1 tablespoon cherry preserves, divided
1⅓ cups all-purpose flour
1¼ teaspoons baking powder
¼ teaspoon kosher salt
½ cup whole buttermilk
Cherry Frosting (recipe follows), divided
Pink food coloring
8 ounces white fondant
Confectioners' sugar, for dusting
1 cup dark chocolate morsels
Garnish: edible luster spray

• Preheat oven to 350°. Spray an 8-inch square cake pan with baking spray with flour. Line pan with parchment paper, letting excess extend over sides of pan.
• In the bowl of a stand mixer fitted with the paddle attachment, beat together butter and granulated sugar at medium speed until light and fluffy, 3 to 4 minutes, stopping to scrape sides of bowl. Add eggs, one at a time, beating well with each addition. Add vanilla bean paste and 1 tablespoon cherry preserves, beating until combined.
• In a medium bowl, whisk together flour, baking powder, and salt. With mixer at low speed, gradually add flour mixture to butter mixture alternately with buttermilk, beginning and ending with flour mixture, beating just until combined with each addition. Spoon batter into prepared pan.
• Bake until a wooden pick inserted in center comes out clean, 25 to 35 minutes. Let cool in pan for 10 minutes. Remove from pan, and let cool completely on a wire rack. Wrap cake in plastic wrap, and refrigerate overnight.
• Using a sharp knife or a 2¼-inch square cutter, cut 16 squares from cake. Using a serrated knife, cut each cake square in half horizontally.
• Place approximately ⅔ cup Cherry Frosting in a piping bag fitted with a small round tip (Wilton #805). Pipe a border of frosting onto bottom half of each cake square. Spoon ¼ teaspoon cherry preserves inside each frosting border. Cover with top half of each cake square. Freeze cake squares for 20 minutes.
• Using a miniature offset spatula, spread a thin layer of remaining Cherry Frosting onto each cake, creating a smooth, even layer. Refrigerate cakes for 20 minutes.
• Knead desired amount of pink food coloring into fondant until color is fully incorporated. Place fondant on a confectioners' sugar-dusted surface. Using a rolling pin, roll out fondant to a ¹⁄₁₆-inch thickness.

• Using a sharp knife, cut fondant into 16 (5-inch) squares. Cover fondant with plastic wrap to prevent drying out.
• Drape a fondant square over each cake square. Use fingers to smooth out fondant on top of cake, working down sides of cake and moving fingers over fondant with even pressure. Trim and discard excess fondant from bottom of each cake.
• Using a small flower-shaped cookie cutter, cut 16 flowers from fondant. If desired, bend petals of fondant flowers slightly to cup.
• In a medium heatproof bowl, warm chocolate in microwave oven on high in 30-second intervals, stirring between each, until chocolate melts.
• Dip bottom of each cake square in melted chocolate. Place cakes on parchment paper until chocolate sets.
• Using a very small food-safe brush or a wooden pick, place a dot of remaining melted chocolate on rounded side of each fondant flower to adhere to cake squares, and place a smaller dot of melted chocolate in center of curved side of each flower. Spray cakes with edible luster spray, if desired.
• Store petits fours in an airtight container, and refrigerate for up to 3 days.

Cherry Frosting

Makes 2 cups

1 cup unsalted butter, softened
3⅔ cups confectioners' sugar
1 tablespoon heavy whipping cream
2 teaspoons cherry preserves

• In the bowl of a stand mixer fitted with the paddle attachment, beat butter at medium speed until light and creamy, 3 to 4 minutes. With mixer at low speed, add confectioners' sugar, 1 cup at a time, stopping to scrape sides of bowl after each addition. Add cream and cherry preserves, beating until combined. Use immediately.

Strawberry & Mango Mochi Balls
Makes 12

1 pint strawberry ice cream, divided
1 pint mango ice cream, divided
1½ cups water, divided
1 cup plus 3 tablespoons granulated sugar,
   divided
1 cup rice flour, divided
⅛ teaspoon strawberry extract
Pink food coloring
Potato starch, for dusting
Yellow food coloring
Orange food coloring

• Place a 12-well silicone miniature muffin pan on
a rimmed baking sheet. Place in freezer.
• Line wells of a 12-well metal miniature muffin pan
with plastic wrap.
• Using a levered 2-teaspoon scoop, place a scoop
of strawberry ice cream in 6 of the 12 wells of frozen
silicone muffin pan, and place a scoop of mango ice
cream in each of the remaining 6 wells. Return to freezer.
• In a medium heatproof bowl, whisk together ¾ cup
water, ½ cup plus 1½ tablespoons sugar, ½ cup rice flour,
strawberry extract, and desired amount of pink food
coloring. Microwave on high for 1½ minutes. Stir mixture
until combined. Microwave 1 minute more. (Mixture
should be shiny and look like a paste.)
• Turn out dough onto a heavily potato starch–covered
surface. Knead gently until dough comes together
completely. Using a rolling pin, roll out dough into an
11x10-inch rectangle. Using a sharp knife, cut 6 (3-inch)
squares from dough.
• Store dough squares in an airtight container with plastic
wrap between each layer. Refrigerate for at least 1 hour.
• In a medium heatproof bowl, whisk together remaining
¾ cup water, remaining ½ cup plus 1½ tablespoons
sugar, remaining ½ cup rice flour, and desired amount
of yellow and orange food coloring to achieve a mango
color. Microwave on high for 1½ minutes. Stir mixture
until combined. Microwave 1 minute more. (Mixture
should be shiny and look like a paste.)
• Turn out dough onto a heavily potato starch–covered
surface. Knead gently until dough comes together
completely. Using a rolling pin, roll out dough into an
11x10-inch rectangle. Using a sharp knife, cut 6 (3-inch)
squares from dough.
• Store dough squares in an airtight container with plastic
wrap between each layer. Refrigerate for at least 1 hour.
• Place a dough square in each prepared well of metal

muffin pan. Working quickly, one scoop at a time, place
an ice cream portion from silicone muffin pan in center
of a dough square (strawberry ice cream on pink squares;
mango ice cream on yellow squares). Fold corners of
dough into center to encase ice cream, and pinch ends
to seal. Wrap dough balls in plastic wrap, and twist to
maintain a round shape. Invert metal muffin pan, and
place wrapped balls on top of muffin cups, rounded side
up. Place in freezer. Freeze for at least 8 hours before
serving. Remove plastic wrap before serving.

Matcha-Lemon Cookies
Makes 104 *(photo on page 64)*

¾ cup plus 2 tablespoons unsalted butter, softened
⅓ cup plus 1 teaspoon confectioners' sugar
4 large egg yolks, divided
2½ teaspoons fresh lemon zest, divided
1½ teaspoons matcha powder
¼ teaspoon vanilla bean paste
¼ teaspoon kosher salt
2 cups plus 1 tablespoon all-purpose flour
3 cups granulated sugar

• In the bowl of a stand mixer fitted with the paddle
attachment, beat together butter and confectioners'
sugar at medium-low speed until light and creamy,
3 to 4 minutes, stopping to scrape sides of bowl. Add
1 egg yolk, ½ teaspoon lemon zest, matcha powder,
vanilla bean paste, and salt, and beat together until fully
incorporated. Scrape sides of bowl. Add flour, beating
until dough comes together.
• Turn out dough onto a heavily floured surface. Divide
dough into 4 equal portions. Roll each dough portion
into a 13x½-inch log, and roll up each log in parchment
paper, ending seam side down and tucking ends under.
Refrigerate overnight.
• Preheat oven to 350°. Line several rimmed baking
sheets with parchment paper.
• Let dough sit at room temperature for 5 minutes.
• In a 13x9-inch dish or pan, combine granulated sugar
and remaining 2 teaspoons lemon zest, stirring well.
• In a small bowl, whisk remaining 3 egg yolks, and brush
thinly onto dough logs. Roll dough logs in lemon sugar.
• Using a sharp knife, cut dough into ½-inch slices. Place
slices ½ inch apart on prepared baking sheets.
• Bake cookies until edges are just beginning to brown,
7 to 8 minutes. Remove cookies from baking sheets, and
let cool completely on wire racks. Store in an airtight
container at room temperature for up to 5 days.

Morocco

In the North African country of Morocco, drinking Maghrebi mint tea is a part of daily life. This green tea, prepared with mint leaves and sometimes sugar, is a popular custom and often savored multiple times per day. There is even a Moroccan saying about the libation: "The first glass is as bitter as life; the second glass is as strong as love; the third glass is as gentle as death." Offering mint tea to guests is a sign of good hospitality, and the preparation of the infusion is usually entrusted only to senior family members.

Served from fanciful glass or brass teapots into beautifully adorned tall glasses, this brisk beverage pairs delightfully with teatime treats infused with traditional Moroccan spices and inspired by the rich, bold flavors of the nation's cuisine. From the scones course, which incorporates a fragrant spice mixture, to a hearty savories course with variations on classic Moroccan fare, to the decadent sweets course accented with touches of almond, rosewater, and lemon, this vibrant menu brings flavorful morsels from North Africa to your tea table.

The MENU

SCONE
Moroccan Spice Scones
Organic Moroccan Mint

SAVORIES
Sardine Salad Sandwiches
Zaalouk Canapés
Chicken Tagine
Organic Gunpowder Green

SWEETS
Nectarine-Pistachio Ktefa
(Layered Moroccan Pastry)
Kaab el Ghazal
(Gazelle Horn Cookies)
Lemon-Coconut Basbousa
Sailor's Delight

Tea Pairings by Capital Teas,
888-484-8327, capitalteas.com

"To a Moroccan, mint tea is a ritual of good hospitality and daily life."

—James Norwood Pratt,
James Norwood Pratt's Tea Dictionary

Moroccan Spice Scones
Makes 8

2 cups all-purpose flour
⅓ cup granulated sugar
1 tablespoon Ras El Hanout Spice Mixture
   (recipe follows)
2 teaspoons baking powder
½ teaspoon salt
¼ cup cold unsalted butter
¾ cup plus 3 tablespoons cold
   heavy whipping cream, divided
½ teaspoon vanilla extract

• Preheat oven to 350º. Line a rimmed baking sheet with
parchment paper.
• In a large bowl, whisk together flour, sugar, Ras El
Hanout Spice Mixture, baking powder, and salt. Using
a pastry blender or 2 forks, cut in cold butter until it
resembles coarse crumbs.
• In a small bowl, stir together ¾ cup plus 2 tablespoons
cold cream and vanilla extract. Add cream mixture
to flour mixture, stirring until evenly moist. (If dough
seems dry, add more cream, 1 tablespoon at a time.)
Working gently, bring mixture together with hands
until a dough forms.
• Turn out dough onto a lightly floured surface, and
knead gently 4 to 5 times. Using a rolling pin, roll out
dough to a 1-inch thickness. Using a 2¼-inch hexagonal
cutter, cut 8 scones from dough, rerolling scraps as
necessary. Place scones 2 inches apart on prepared
baking sheet. Brush top of scones with remaining
1 tablespoon cold cream.
• Bake until edges of scones are golden brown and
a wooden pick inserted in centers comes out clean,
approximately 20 minutes. Serve warm.

Ras El Hanout Spice Mixture
Makes ¼ cup

½ teaspoon anise seed
½ teaspoon whole coriander seed
2 teaspoons ground ginger
1 teaspoon ground cinnamon
1 teaspoon ground turmeric
½ teaspoon ground cardamom
½ teaspoon ground allspice
½ teaspoon ground mace
¼ teaspoon ground nutmeg
¼ teaspoon ground white pepper
⅛ teaspoon ground cloves

RECOMMENDED CONDIMENTS
• Sweetened Whipped Cream
• Orange Marmalade

• Using a mortar and pestle or an electric spice grinder,
grind anise seed and coriander seed to a fine texture.
• In a small bowl, whisk together ground seed mixture,
ginger, cinnamon, turmeric, cardamom, allspice, mace,
nutmeg, white pepper, and cloves until thoroughly
combined. Store in an airtight container away from heat
and light until needed.

Sweetened Whipped Cream
Makes 1¼ cups

¾ cup cold heavy whipping cream
1 tablespoon confectioners' sugar

• In a deep bowl, beat together cream and confectioners'
sugar with a mixer at high speed until light and fluffy.

Sardine Salad Sandwiches
Makes 16

1 (3.75-ounce) can sardines in olive oil, drained
2 tablespoons Chermoula (recipe follows)
8 slices firm white sandwich bread

• In a small bowl, flake sardines into small pieces. Add Chermoula, stirring until combined. Spread sardine mixture onto 4 bread slices. Top with remaining bread slices.
• Using a serrated bread knife, trim and discard crusts from sandwiches. Cut each sandwich diagonally into 4 equal triangles. Serve immediately, or cover with damp paper towels until ready to serve.

Chermoula
Makes ⅓ cup

1 clove garlic, finely chopped
½ teaspoon salt
2 cups fresh parsley leaves, finely chopped
1 cup fresh cilantro leaves, finely chopped
1 teaspoon ground paprika
1 teaspoon ground cumin
½ teaspoon coriander seed
⅛ teaspoon saffron threads
¼ cup plus 1 to 3 tablespoons extra-virgin olive oil
2 tablespoons fresh lemon juice

• Using a mortar and pestle, grind garlic and salt to a purée. Gradually add parsley and cilantro, grinding until a purée forms. Add paprika, cumin, coriander seed, and saffron, grinding until incorporated. Add ¼ cup oil and lemon juice, stirring until combined. Transfer mixture to a covered glass jar, and add remaining 1 to 3 tablespoons oil to cover top of mixture. Refrigerate until needed.

Zaalouk Canapés
Makes 24

3 cups diced peeled eggplant
2 cups diced plum tomatoes
⅓ cup water
¼ cup loosely packed fresh cilantro leaves
¼ cup loosely packed fresh parsley leaves
¼ cup plus 1 tablespoon extra-virgin olive oil, divided
2 cloves garlic, finely chopped
1 tablespoon ground paprika
1 tablespoon ground cumin
1 teaspoon salt
1 tablespoon fresh lemon juice
6 large pita breads
Garnish: chopped fresh parsley

• In a medium deep sauté pan, bring eggplant, tomatoes, ⅓ cup water, cilantro, parsley, ¼ cup oil, garlic, paprika, cumin, and salt to a boil over high heat. Reduce heat to medium; cover and cook, stirring occasionally, until vegetables are tender and broken down, approximately 30 minutes.
• Using a potato masher, crush and blend vegetables. Add lemon juice, stirring to combine. Cook, uncovered, until mixture thickens.
• Preheat oven to 350°. Line a rimmed baking sheet with parchment paper.
• Using a 1¾-inch round cutter, cut 24 circles from pita breads. Place on prepared baking sheet. Brush top of pita rounds lightly with remaining 1 tablespoon oil.
• Bake until crisp and lightly browned, 5 to 7 minutes. Let cool.
• Spoon a small amount of vegetable mixture onto pita rounds.
• Garnish with parsley, if desired. Serve immediately.

Chicken Tagine
Makes 8 servings

2 boneless skinless chicken breasts
   (approximately 1 pound)
½ tablespoon Ras El Hanout Spice Mixture
   (recipe on page 73)
¼ teaspoon salt
2 tablespoons extra-virgin olive oil
1 cup sliced yellow onion
½ tablespoon finely minced garlic
¼ cup fresh cilantro leaves, chopped
¼ cup fresh parsley leaves, chopped
¼ cup pimiento-stuffed olives, sliced
¼ cup kalamata olives, sliced
¼ cup chicken broth
2 tablespoons chopped preserved lemon
4 cups hot cooked couscous

• Using a sharp knife, cut chicken into bite-size pieces. Sprinkle with Ras El Hanout Spice Mixture and salt.
• In a small Dutch oven or braiser, heat oil over medium-high heat. Add chicken; reduce heat to medium. Sear chicken on all sides until very lightly browned. Remove chicken, and set aside. Add onion and garlic; cook, stirring occasionally, until onions are slightly tender and very lightly browned. Add cilantro, parsley, olives, broth, and preserved lemon; reduce heat to low. Cover and simmer until chicken and onions are very tender and moist, 1 hour to 1½ hours. (Check stew occasionally to make sure broth has not cooked out. If needed, add broth to keep mixture moist.) Serve over hot cooked couscous.

- Preheat oven to 350º. Line 2 rimmed baking sheets with parchment paper.
- Lay a phyllo dough sheet on top of parchment paper. Lightly spray phyllo with cooking spray. Sprinkle with cinnamon sugar. Repeat procedure with 2 more phyllo dough sheets, creating 3 layers of phyllo. Lay another parchment paper sheet on top of phyllo dough. Place a baking sheet on top of parchment paper to weigh down phyllo while baking. Repeat with remaining phyllo dough in second prepared baking sheet.
- Bake until phyllo sheets are deep golden brown, approximately 10 minutes. Let cool completely.
- When cool, cut each phyllo sheet into 12 (3-inch) squares. Place a phyllo square onto a dessert plate. Spread with a thin layer of Rosewater Pastry Cream. Top with nectarines, pistachios, and another phyllo square. Spread another thin layer of Rosewater Pastry Cream. Top with nectarines, pistachios, and a third phyllo square, creating a triple stack. Repeat with remaining ingredients to create 8 triple stacks.
- Garnish with rose petals and pistachios, if desired. Serve immediately.

Rose petals used for culinary purposes should be pesticide free. Edible rose petals are available from Gourmet Sweet Botanicals, gourmetsweetbotanicals.com.

Rosewater Pastry Cream
Makes 1 cup

¾ cup whole milk
2 large egg yolks
2 tablespoons granulated sugar
1½ tablespoons cornstarch
½ teaspoon culinary rosewater*
1 teaspoon unsalted butter

- In a small saucepan, heat milk until hot and steaming, but not boiling.
- In a small bowl, whisk together egg yolks, sugar, and cornstarch. Gradually add hot milk, whisking constantly. Return milk mixture to saucepan. Cook over medium heat, whisking constantly, until mixture thickens and comes to a simmer. Remove from heat. Add rosewater and butter, whisking until incorporated.
- Pour mixture through a fine-mesh sieve into a heatproof bowl. Cover surface of pastry cream with plastic wrap, and refrigerate for at least 6 hours or overnight.

We used Al Wadi Rose Water.

Nectarine-Pistachio Ktefa (Layered Moroccan Pastry)
Makes 8

6 (14x9-inch) sheets phyllo dough
¼ cup cinnamon sugar
Rosewater Pastry Cream (recipe follows)
1 cup finely chopped nectarines
⅓ cup finely chopped roasted salted pistachios
Garnish: fresh edible rose petals*, finely chopped roasted salted pistachios

Kaab el Ghazal
(Gazelle Horn Cookies)
Makes 40

3 cups all-purpose flour
¾ cup unsalted butter, melted
2½ large eggs*, divided
½ teaspoon salt
2 (8-ounce) packages almond paste
¼ cup plus 1 tablespoon culinary orange
    flower water†, divided
2 cups confectioners' sugar
    Garnish: additional confectioners' sugar

• Preheat oven to 350º. Line 2 rimmed baking sheets with parchment paper.
• In the bowl of a stand mixer fitted with the paddle attachment, beat together flour, melted butter, 1½ eggs, and salt at medium speed until combined. (Mixture will be thick.) Switch to the dough hook attachment, and beat for 5 minutes.
• Turn out dough onto a lightly floured surface, and knead by hand for 5 minutes, folding dough over and giving it quarter turns. (Dough will be very firm but smooth and somewhat elastic.) Divide dough into 4 portions. Wrap each portion in plastic wrap, and let rest for 15 minutes.
• While dough is resting, roll almond paste into 40 (2x½-inch) logs. Keep covered with plastic wrap to prevent drying out.
• Using a rolling pin and working with one portion of dough at a time on a lightly floured surface, roll out dough to a ¹⁄₁₆-inch thickness. Using a sharp knife, cut dough into 10 (3x2-inch) rectangles. Place an almond paste log in center of dough rectangle. Roll up dough firmly and evenly to encase almond log, ending with seam side down. Pinch and taper dough at ends, and form into a crescent shape. Place 2 inches apart on prepared baking sheets. Repeat with remaining dough portions.
• In a small bowl, whisk together remaining egg and 1 tablespoon orange flower water until combined. Brush cookies with mixture. Using a wooden pick, prick 3 holes along top of each cookie.
• Bake until edges are very light golden brown, approximately 12 minutes. While cookies are still warm, sprinkle lightly with remaining ¼ cup orange flower water, and roll in confectioners' sugar. Place cookies on wire racks, and let cool completely. Store in an airtight container at room temperature with layers separated by wax paper.
• Just before serving, garnish with a dusting of additional confectioners' sugar, if desired.

*To measure ½ of an egg, lightly beat with a fork, and then measure in a liquid-measuring cup, using half the portion.
†We used Al Wadi Orange Blossom Water.

Lemon-Coconut Basbousa
Makes 40 cake squares

1⅓ cups semolina flour
¾ cup granulated sugar
½ cup almond flour
⅓ cup minced dried unsweetened coconut
½ teaspoon baking soda
¼ teaspoon baking powder
¼ teaspoon ground cardamom
⅛ teaspoon salt
½ cup whole buttermilk
¼ cup butter, melted
40 Marcona almonds
Lemon Syrup (recipe follows)

• Preheat oven to 350º. Line an 8-inch square baking pan with foil, letting excess extend over sides of pan. Lightly spray with cooking spray.
• In a large bowl, whisk together semolina flour, sugar, almond flour, coconut, baking soda, baking powder, cardamom, and salt. With a mixer at medium speed, beat together flour mixture, buttermilk, and melted butter until batter is very thick.
• Using an offset spatula, spread batter into prepared pan, creating a level surface. Using a sharp knife, score parallel lines into batter diagonally, creating 40 (1¼-inch) diamond shapes. Place an almond in center of each diamond.
• Bake until edges are golden brown and a wooden pick inserted in center comes out clean, 40 minutes. Immediately pour Lemon Syrup over cake, and let soak into cake. Transfer pan to a wire rack, and let cake cool completely. Cover pan with plastic wrap, and refrigerate overnight.
• Place cake on a cutting surface. Using a long sharp knife, cut cake into diamond-shaped pieces following scored lines.

Lemon Syrup
Makes ¾ cup

½ cup granulated sugar
½ cup water
6 lemon slices

• In a small saucepan, bring sugar and ½ cup water to a boil over medium-high heat. Reduce heat to low. Add lemon slices; simmer for 10 minutes. Remove lemons. Let syrup cool to room temperature before using.

Netherlands

The Dutch East India Company had the special distinction of introducing tea to Europe with imports from China in 1610. Over the centuries that followed, the country's appetite for the beverage unfortunately waned gradually. Recently, there has been a resurgence of interest in tea, resulting in a marvelous growth of tea shops, tea companies, and even tea plants.

Pay tribute to the Netherlands' important role in tea history with a menu that features iconic Dutch ingredients like gouda, herring, and chocolate in the various courses for a lovely afternoon tea structured in the familiar European order: savories, scones, and sweets. Snert, a green pea soup, is accompanied by hearty canapés of potato, sausage, and sauerkraut. Barely sweet rye scones are delicious topped with ligonberry preserves and teapot-shaped speculaas, colorful tampões, and rich oliebollen are traditional treats that make for a memorable finale. From the dinnerware to the linens, adorn the table with blue and white in homage to Delftware, the pottery for which the Netherlands is so well known. A bright arrangement of fresh tulips also pays a respectful nod to the famous flowers found each year in Holland from mid-April to early May and exported to many parts of the world.

The MENU

SAVORIES
Potato, Sausage, and
Sauerkraut Canapés
Pickled Herring Tea Sandwiches
Green Pea Soup
Ceylon New Vithanakande Black

SCONE
Rye and Gouda Scones
Osmanthus Dragon Pearls Green

SWEETS
Oliebollen
(Chocolate Doughnut Balls)
Speculaas Teapot Cookies
Tompões
Orange Black

*Tea Pairings by Global Tea Mart,
844-208-2337, globalteamart.com*

Potato, Sausage, and Sauerkraut Canapés
Makes 8

2 large russet potatoes, peeled and cubed
½ teaspoon salt
2 tablespoons whole milk
2 tablespoons unsalted butter, divided
1 tablespoon plus 1 teaspoon spicy brown mustard
½ cup chopped cooked beef sausage
½ cup sauerkraut, well drained

• Preheat oven to 425º.
• In a medium saucepan, bring potatoes, salt, and enough water to cover to a boil over medium-high heat. Boil gently until potatoes are tender when pierced with a fork, approximately 10 minutes. Drain well.
• Transfer potatoes to a heatproof bowl. Add milk and 1 tablespoon butter, and beat with a mixer at high speed until light and fluffy.
• While potato mixture is still warm, transfer it to a piping bag fitted with large open-star tip (Wilton #1M). Working in concentric circles, pipe potato mixture into 8 rounds directly onto an ungreased rimmed baking sheet. Pipe 1 to 2 extra layers onto perimeters to form a rim around the edge of each round. Drizzle remaining 1 tablespoon butter onto rounds.
• Bake until potato rounds are set and lightly browned, 15 to 20 minutes. Remove from oven, and transfer potato rounds to a serving platter.
• Divide mustard, sausage, and sauerkraut among warm potato rounds. Serve immediately.

Pickled Herring Tea Sandwiches
Makes 9

1 (8-ounce) package cream cheese, softened
½ cup chopped pickled herring
2 tablespoons chopped dill pickle
1 tablespoon chopped sweet onion
⅛ teaspoon ground black pepper
9 very thin slices wheat bread

• In a medium bowl, stir cream cheese until soft and creamy. Add herring, dill pickle, onion, and pepper, stirring until combined.
• Spread an even layer of cream cheese mixture onto 2 bread slices. Stack a bread slice, cream cheese side up, onto other bread slice, cream cheese side up. Cover with a plain bread slice to create a triple-stack sandwich. Repeat with remaining bread slices and remaining cream cheese mixture to create a total of 3 triple-stack sandwiches.

• Using a serrated bread knife, trim and discard crusts from sandwiches. Cut each sandwich into 3 rectangles. Serve immediately, or cover with damp paper towels, place in a covered containter, and refrigerate until serving time.

Snert (Green Pea Soup)
Makes 6 servings

1 tablespoon olive oil
½ cup finely chopped leek
¼ cup finely chopped celery
2 tablespoons finely chopped carrot
4 cups unsalted chicken broth
1 cup dried split green peas
½ teaspoon salt
Garnish: chopped celery leaves

• In a large saucepan, heat oil over medium-high heat. Add leek, celery, and carrot; reduce heat to medium-low. Cook, stirring frequently, until vegetables are tender, 3 to 5 minutes. Add broth, peas, and salt; cook, stirring occasionally, until peas are tender, 30 to 40 minutes. (Soup will be fairly thick, as is typical in the Netherlands.) Serve hot.
• Garnish individual servings with celery leaves, if desired.

MAKE-AHEAD TIP: Soup can be made a day in advance, stored in a covered container, and refrigerated. Reheat gently in a saucepan. For a thinner consistency, add more chicken broth, if desired.

• Lingonberry Preserves

Rye and Gouda Scones
Makes 12

1½ cups dark rye flour*
1 cup all-purpose flour
1 tablespoon baking powder
1 teaspoon granulated sugar
½ teaspoon salt
¼ cup cold unsalted butter
1 cup shredded Gouda cheese
1¼ cups plus 3 tablespoons cold heavy whipping
   cream, divided

• Preheat oven to 375º. Line a rimmed baking sheet with parchment paper.
• In a large bowl, whisk together rye flour, all-purpose flour, baking powder, sugar, and salt. Using a pastry blender or 2 forks, cut in cold butter until mixture resembles coarse crumbs. Add cheese, stirring until combined. Add 1¼ cups plus 2 tablespoons cold cream, stirring until evenly moist. (If dough seems dry, add more

cream, 1 tablespoon at a time.) Working gently, bring mixture together with hands until a dough forms.
• Turn out dough onto a lightly floured surface, and knead gently 4 to 5 times. Using a rolling pin, roll out dough to a 1-inch thickness. Using a 2¼-inch round cutter, cut 12 scones from dough, rerolling scraps as necessary. Place scones 2 inches apart on prepared baking sheet. Brush top of scones with remaining 1 tablespoon cold cream.
• Bake until edges of scones are browned and a wooden pick inserted in centers comes out clean, 18 to 20 minutes. Serve warm.

*We used Bob's Red Mill Whole Grain Stone Ground Rye Flour.

Oliebollen (Chocolate Doughnut Balls)
Makes 100

½ cup warm water (105° to 110º)
¼ cup plus 1 teaspoon granulated sugar, divided
2 (0.25-ounce) packages dry active yeast
3½ cups all-purpose flour
½ cup Dutch process cocoa powder
1 teaspoon salt
2 large eggs
2 cups whole milk, room temperature
8 cups vegetable oil
Garnish: confectioners' sugar

• In a small bowl, stir together ½ cup warm water and 1 teaspoon granulated sugar. Sprinkle yeast on top. Let stand until mixture is foamy, approximately 10 minutes.
• In a large bowl, sift together flour, cocoa, salt, and remaining ¼ cup granulated sugar. Make a well in center of flour mixture; add eggs, yeast mixture, and 1 cup milk, stirring until well combined. Add remaining 1 cup milk, stirring well. (If mixture is lumpy, whisk until fairly smooth.) Cover bowl with a damp dish towel. Let rise in a warm, draft-free place (75°) until doubled in size, approximately 1 hour. Stir dough down. (Dough will be very sticky.)
• Line several rimmed baking sheets with paper towels.
• In a deep saucepan or Dutch oven, heat oil over medium heat until a deep-fry thermometer registers 350º. Dip a levered 2-teaspoon scoop or 2 small spoons into hot oil to coat. Scoop out balls of dough, and carefully drop into hot oil in batches, 6 to 8 balls at a time. Fry until doughnut balls look firm, 3 to 4 minutes. Remove using a slotted spoon, and place on prepared baking sheets.
• To garnish, toss warm doughnut balls in confectioners' sugar, if desired.
• Serve warm or at room temperature.

Speculaas Teapot Cookies
Makes 44

½ cup unsalted butter, softened
⅓ cup granulated sugar
¾ cup firmly packed dark brown sugar
1 large egg
1½ teaspoon vanilla extract
1¾ cups all-purpose flour
1½ teaspoons ground cinnamon
½ teaspoon ground ginger
½ teaspoon ground coriander
½ teaspoon ground anise
½ teaspoon salt
¼ teaspoon ground white pepper
¼ teaspoon baking soda
¼ teaspoon ground nutmeg
¼ teaspoon ground cloves
¼ teaspoon ground cardamom

• Preheat oven to 375º. Line several rimmed baking sheets with parchment paper.

• In a large bowl, beat together butter and sugars with a mixer at medium speed until fluffy, 3 to 4 minutes, stopping to scrape sides of bowl. Add egg and vanilla extract, beating until incorporated.

• In a medium bowl, whisk together flour, cinnamon, ginger, coriander, anise, salt, white pepper, baking soda, nutmeg, cloves, and cardamom. With mixer on low speed, gradually add flour mixture to butter mixture, beating until a dough forms.

• Divide dough into 2 portions. Place each dough portion between 2 sheets of wax paper. Using a rolling pin, roll dough to a ⅛-inch thickness. Keep dough portions between wax paper, and place onto baking sheets. Freeze for 15 minutes.

• Working with one frozen dough portion at a time, remove top wax paper layer, and using a teapot-shaped cutter, cut 22 cookies from each portion, rerolling scraps as necessary. Working quickly so dough remains firm, place cookies 2 inches apart on prepared baking sheets.

• Bake until edges of cookies are golden brown, approximately 10 minutes. Remove cookies from baking sheets, and let cool completely on wire racks. Store in an airtight container with layers separated by wax paper.

Tompões
Makes 18

1 (17.3-ounce) package frozen puff pastry,
  slightly thawed
1 large egg
1 tablespoon water
Pink Glaze (recipe follows)
Vanilla Pastry Cream (recipe follows)
Sweetened Whipped Cream (recipe follows)

• Preheat oven to 400°. Line 2 rimmed baking sheets
with parchment paper.
• On a lightly floured surface, unfold puff pastry
sheets. Using a sharp knife, cut dough into 9 (3x2-inch)
rectangles. Place on prepared baking sheets.
In a small bowl, whisk together egg and 1 tablespoon
water. Brush egg wash on top of puff pastry rectangles.
• Bake puff pastry rectangles until puffed and golden
brown, 13 to 15 minutes. Let cool.
• Dip top of baked puffs into Pink Glaze, letting excess
drip off so that glaze does not run when pastry is turned
over. Let glaze dry.
• Using a serrated knife, cut puffs in half horizontally,
being careful not to disturb glaze.
• Place Vanilla Pastry Cream in a piping bag fitted with
a large round tip (Wilton #1A). Pipe Vanilla Pastry Cream
onto bottom half of puffs. Cover with top half of puffs.
• Place Sweetened Whipped Cream in a piping bag
fitting with a large open-star tip (Wilton #1M). Pipe a
stripe of Sweetened Whipped Cream on top of glaze.

Pink Glaze
Makes ½ cup

1 cup confectioners' sugar
5 teaspoons whole milk
Pink paste food coloring

• In a deep bowl, whisk together confectioners' sugar and
milk. Add desired amount food coloring to achieve a pink
color. (If glaze is too runny, add additional confectioners'
sugar, a small amount at a time. If mixture is too thick,
add additional milk, a very small amount at a time.)

Vanilla Pastry Cream
Makes 1¾ cups

2 cups whole milk
4 large egg yolks
½ cup granulated sugar
3 tablespoons cornstarch
⅛ teaspoon salt
1 tablespoon unsalted butter
1 teaspoon vanilla extract

• In a medium saucepan, heat milk over medium-high
heat until very hot.
• In a medium bowl, whisk together egg yolks and
sugar. Gradually add hot milk to egg mixture, whisking
constantly. Add cornstarch and salt, whisking until
incorporated. Strain mixture through a fine-mesh sieve.
Return mixture to saucepan. Cook over medium heat,
whisking constantly, until mixture thickens. Add butter
and vanilla extract, whisking well.
• Transfer pastry cream to a heatproof container. Cover
with a piece of plastic wrap, pressing wrap directly onto
surface of pastry cream to prevent a skin from forming.
Refrigerate until very cold, at least 4 hours or overnight.

Sweetened Whipped Cream
Makes 1¼ cups

¾ cup cold heavy whipping cream
1 tablespoon confectioners' sugar

• In a deep bowl, beat together cream and confectioners'
sugar with a mixer at high speed until light and fluffy.

Russia

Tea has been part of Russian culture since the late 1600s, when tea leaves were said to have first come to Russia by camel from China through Mongolia, a journey that often took as long as 16 months. Initially available only to the wealthy, the beverage has since become quite affordable and remains a staple for all classes in the cold-climate country. The samovar, meaning "self boiler," was developed to heat water for tea. Fashioned of metal and often featuring a chimney for keeping hot a pot of tea concentrate, samovars can be rather simple or elaborately decorated and are now used in other parts of the world as well.

A table set with an elegant, Russian-made porcelain tea service is the perfect backdrop for a menu of scones, savories, and sweets that all incorporate ingredients popular in the nation's traditional cuisine. Borscht soup, pirozhki, and smoked salmon and caviar–topped blinis comprise the hearty savories course. Afternoon-tea guests will delight when served individual-size honey cakes, Tula pryanik (a gingerbread variation from the Russian city where samovars originated), and pastila candies made with honey and green apple. Make sure to have a samovar heated and ready for guests to enjoy endless cups of tea.

"A samovar is singing."

—Russian Proverb

The MENU

SCONE
Sour Cream & Chocolate Scones
Mountain-Grown Fancy Ceylon

SAVORIES
Borscht Soup
**Smoked Salmon, Caviar &
Buckwheat Blini Canapés**
Pirozhki (Mini Pies)
*Russian Caravan Original
China Blend*

SWEETS
Sour Apple & Honey Pastila (Pastels)
Tula (Russian Gingerbread)
Russian Honey Cakes
First Flush Darjeeling

*Tea Pairings by Grace Tea Company,
978-635-9500, gracetea.com*

RECOMMENDED
CONDIMENT
_____

• Vanilla Custard

Sour Cream & Chocolate Scones
Makes 12

1½ cups all-purpose flour
½ cup bread flour
2 tablespoons granulated sugar
1 tablespoon baking powder
1 teaspoon kosher salt
¼ cup plus 1 tablespoon cold unsalted butter, cubed
1 cup sour cream
½ cup milk chocolate morsels
1 large egg
1 teaspoon heavy whipping cream

• Preheat oven to 425°. Line a rimmed baking sheet with parchment paper.
• In the work bowl of a food processor, pulse together both flours, sugar, baking powder, and salt. Add cold butter, and pulse until mixture resembles coarse crumbs. Transfer dough to a large bowl. Add sour cream and chocolate, stirring until combined.
• Turn out dough onto a lightly floured surface, and gently knead 4 to 5 times. Using a rolling pin, roll out dough to a ¾-inch thickness. Using a 2-inch fluted round cutter, cut 12 scones from dough, rerolling scraps as necessary. Place scones 2 inches apart on prepared baking sheet.
• In a small bowl, whisk together egg and cream. Brush top of scones with egg mixture.
• Bake until edges of scones are golden brown and a wooden pick inserted in centers comes out clean, 12 to 15 minutes. Serve warm.

Vanilla Custard
Makes 1 cup

¾ cup whole milk
⅓ cup heavy whipping cream
1 vanilla bean, split, seeds scraped and reserved
4 large egg yolks
¼ cup granulated sugar
2 tablespoons cornstarch
½ teaspoon kosher salt
1 tablespoon unsalted butter, softened

• In a medium saucepan, bring milk, cream, and vanilla bean and reserved seeds to a boil over medium heat. Remove from heat.
• In a medium bowl, whisk together egg yolks, sugar, cornstarch, and salt. Gradually add hot milk mixture to egg mixture, whisking constantly. Strain milk mixture back into saucepan, and cook over medium heat, whisking constantly, until thickened.
• Transfer custard to a medium bowl. Add butter, stirring well. Cover surface of custard with a piece of plastic wrap to prevent a skin from forming. Refrigerate for at least 1 hour and up to 4 days. Serve cold.

Borscht Soup
Makes 6 cups

2 tablespoons olive oil
½ pound boneless beef chuck roast, diced
¼ cup diced tomatoes
1 cup diced yellow onion
2 large cloves garlic, minced
4 cups beef broth, divided
2 bay leaves
1 teaspoon kosher salt
½ teaspoon ground black pepper
⅛ teaspoon ground marjoram
⅛ teaspoon ground ginger
⅛ teaspoon dried thyme
⅛ teaspoon ground allspice
⅛ teaspoon ground cloves
2 cups grated beets
2 cups thinly sliced green cabbage
½ cup thinly sliced carrot
½ cup thinly sliced celery
¼ cup chopped fresh dill
3 tablespoons red wine vinegar
Garnish: sour cream, fresh dill sprigs, fresh thyme sprigs

• In a medium sauté pan, heat oil over medium-high heat. Add beef and tomatoes; cook until beef is browned completely, approximately 4 minutes per side. Reduce to medium heat. Add onion and garlic; cook until onion is translucent, approximately 4 minutes.
• In a 5½-quart Dutch oven, bring beef mixture, 2 cups broth, bay leaves, salt, pepper, marjoram, ginger, thyme, allspice, and cloves to a boil over high heat. Cover and reduce heat to low; cook for 1 hour, stirring occasionally.
• Add beets, cabbage, carrot, celery, and remaining 2 cups broth; cover and simmer until vegetables are tender, approximately 30 minutes. Add dill and vinegar, stirring well. Serve hot.
• Garnish with sour cream, dill sprigs, and thyme sprigs, if desired.

Smoked Salmon, Caviar & Buckwheat Blini Canapés
Makes 24 to 30

1 cup warm water (105° to 110°)
1 cup buckwheat flour, divided
¼ cup plus 2 teaspoons granulated sugar
2¼ teaspoons (1 package) active dry yeast
2½ teaspoons kosher salt, divided
2 cups warm heavy whipping cream
1½ cups all-purpose flour
2 large egg yolks
¼ cup unsalted butter, melted and cooled,
    plus extra for brushing
1 (4-ounce) package smoked salmon
Herbed Cream Spread (recipe follows)
1 (1.75-ounce) container black caviar
Garnish: fresh dill

• In a large bowl, whisk together 1 cup warm water,
¾ cup buckwheat flour, sugar, yeast, and ½ teaspoon salt.
Cover with a piece of plastic wrap, and let rest at room
temperature for 1 hour.
• Add warm cream, all-purpose flour, egg yolks, melted
butter, remaining ¼ cup buckwheat flour, and remaining
2 teaspoons salt to yeast mixture, whisking until
combined and smooth. (Batter will be slightly sticky.)
• Heat a medium nonstick skillet over medium-low heat.
Brush pan with melted butter. Spoon 2 to 3 tablespoons
batter into skillet for each blini. Cook until edges are dry
and bubbles form in center of pancakes, approximately
3 minutes. Turn, and cook until browned, 2 to 3 minutes.
Repeat with remaining batter. Transfer blinis to a serving
plate, and let cool slightly.
• Using a 2-inch round cutter, cut a round from each
blini, discarding scraps. Refrigerate blini rounds in an
airtight container for up to 2 days with layers separated
by wax paper.
• Using a 1½-inch round cutter, cut a round from smoked
salmon for each blini round. Center a salmon round atop
each blini round.
• Place Herbed Cream Spread in a piping bag fitted
with a large open-star tip (Wilton #1M), and pipe
a rosette on salmon rounds. Divide caviar among
canapés. Serve immediately.
• Garnish with dill, if desired.

Herbed Cream Spread
Makes ½ cup

4 ounces cream cheese, softened
2 tablespoons heavy whipping cream
½ teaspoon chopped fresh dill

• In a medium bowl, beat together cream cheese, cream,
and dill with a mixer at medium speed until smooth.
Store in an airtight container, and refrigerate for up to
5 days. Let come to room temperature before using.

Pirozhki (Mini Pies)
Makes 18

2 cups bread flour
½ teaspoon kosher salt
1¼ cups cold unsalted butter, cubed
¼ cup sour cream
¼ cup plus 1 tablespoon water, divided
½ cup tomato chutney
¾ teaspoon dried thyme
½ teaspoon kosher salt
¼ teaspoon ground black pepper
½ pound ground lamb
¾ cup diced small yellow potatoes
¼ cup diced yellow onion
1 teaspoon minced garlic
1 large egg

• In a large bowl, whisk together flour and salt. Using
a pastry blender or 2 forks, cut in cold butter until it
resembles coarse crumbs. Add sour cream and ¼ cup
water, stirring until a dough forms.
• Turn out dough onto a lightly floured surface, and
knead until smooth. Shape dough into a disk, and wrap
in plastic wrap. Refrigerate for 3 to 4 hours. Let stand at
room temperature for 5 minutes before using.
• Preheat oven to 375°. Line 2 rimmed baking sheets
with parchment paper.
• In a large bowl, whisk together tomato chutney, thyme,
salt, and pepper. Add lamb, potatoes, onion, and garlic,
stirring to combine.
• Using a rolling pin, roll out dough to a ¾-inch thickness
on a lightly floured surface. Using a 3¾-inch round cutter,
cut 18 rounds from dough.
• Spoon 2 teaspoons lamb filling onto each round,
slightly off-centered. Brush edges of dough with a thin
layer of water. Fold dough over to encase filling. Gently
press edges of dough to ensure edges adhere. Using a
fork, crimp edges of dough, if desired.
• Transfer pies to prepared baking sheets. Using a sharp
knife, cut 3 slits in top of each pie.
• In a small bowl, whisk together egg and remaining
1 tablespoon water. Brush a thin layer of egg mixture
onto each pie.
• Bake until pies are a deep golden brown, approximately
45 minutes. Remove pies from baking sheets, and let cool
completely on wire racks.

MAKE-AHEAD TIP: Pie dough can be frozen for up
to 3 months when wrapped tightly in plastic wrap
and sealed in a heavy-duty resealable plastic bag.
Let thaw in refrigerator for 24 hours before using.

Sour Apple & Honey Pastila (Pastels)
Makes 30 candies

2½ cups cold water, divided
¾ cup cornstarch
3 cups granulated sugar
2 tablespoons light corn syrup
1 tablespoons honey
1 tablespoon green apple juice
⅛ teaspoon neon green food coloring
Garnish: confectioners' sugar

• Line a 9-inch square metal baking pan with parchment paper, letting excess extend over sides of pan. Butter and flour* parchment.
• In a medium microwave-safe bowl, whisk together ½ cup water and cornstarch until dissolved. Microwave on high until mixture turns opaque and thickens, approximately 3 minutes. Add granulated sugar, 1 cup at a time, stirring well after each addition. Add corn syrup and honey, stirring until combined. Microwave on high in 5 (5-minute) intervals, stirring between each. Add apple juice and food coloring, stirring until desired color is achieved. Pour into prepared pan.
• Cover with a piece of plastic wrap, pressing wrap directly onto surface to prevent a skin from forming. Using an offset spatula, create a smooth surface. Wrap entire pan in plastic wrap, and let cool for at least 6 hours or overnight.
• Gently peel off plastic wrap. Using excess parchment as handles, remove candy from pan. Using a sharp knife, cut into 30 (1½-inch) squares.
• Garnish with a dusting of confectioners' sugar, if desired.
• To prevent candies from sticking together, sprinkle equal parts confectioners' sugar and cornstarch in bottom of an airtight container. Add candies to container, and store at room temperature for up to 1 month.

*If making gluten-free, use gluten-free flour.

Tula Pryanik (Gingerbread)
Makes 24

¼ cup unsalted butter, softened
¼ cup firmly packed dark brown sugar
¼ cup granulated sugar
¼ cup plus 2 teaspoons vegetable oil
¼ cup plus 2 teaspoons honey
1 large egg, at room temperature
2 teaspoons vanilla extract
¾ cup all-purpose flour
¾ cup bread flour
1 teaspoon baking soda

1 teaspoon ground ginger
½ teaspoon kosher salt
½ teaspoon ground cinnamon
¼ teaspoon ground allspice
¼ teaspoon ground cloves
¼ teaspoon ground cardamom
¼ cup ginger cane sugar

• In the bowl of a stand mixer fitted with the paddle attachment, beat together butter, brown sugar, granulated sugar, and oil at medium speed until fluffy, 3 to 4 minutes, stopping to scrape sides of bowl. With mixer at low speed, add honey, egg, and vanilla extract, beating until combined.
• In a medium bowl, whisk together both flours, baking soda, ginger, salt, cinnamon, allspice, cloves, and cardamom. Gradually add flour mixture to butter mixture, beating just until combined. Wrap dough tightly in plastic wrap, and refrigerate for at least 1 hour or up to 3 days.
• Preheat oven to 375°. Sprinkle ½ teaspoon ginger cane sugar into wells of a 24-well candy mold*.
• Using a levered 2-tablespoon scoop, divide dough among wells prepared mold. Press dough into wells to ensure even distribution.
• Bake until edges are lightly browned, 13 to 15 minutes. Let cool slightly before carefully pressing cookies out of molds while still warm. Let cool completely on a wire rack. Store at room temperature in an airtight container with layers separated by wax paper.

*We used a Wilton 24-cavity silicone Daisy Bite-Size Treat Mold.

Russian Honey Cakes
Makes 8

¾ cup granulated sugar
½ cup unsalted butter
¼ cup honey
1 teaspoon baking soda
3 large eggs, lightly beaten
3½ cups all-purpose flour, divided
½ teaspoon ground allspice
½ teaspoon ground cloves
½ teaspoon ground ginger
¼ teaspoon kosher salt
1 teaspoon vanilla extract
Sour Cream Frosting (recipe follows)
Garnish: Chocolate Bees (recipe follows)

• Preheat oven to 350°. Line 3 rimmed baking sheets with parchment paper.
• In a medium saucepan, bring sugar, butter, and honey to a simmer over medium heat. Add baking soda, whisking well. (Mixture will bubble up and drastically change color. Keep whisking until a dark amber color is achieved and mixture is no longer bubbling.) Remove pan from heat. Whisking vigorously, gradually add eggs until combined.
• In a large bowl, whisk together 3 cups flour, allspice, cloves, ginger, and salt. Using a wooden spoon, add flour mixture and vanilla extract to honey mixture, stirring until well combined. Add remaining ½ cup flour, stirring gently just until combined.
• Transfer dough to a parchment paper sheet, and divide into 4 equal portions. Cover with a towel to keep warm.
• Working with one dough portion at a time, lightly sprinkle top with flour, and place on another parchment paper sheet. Using a rolling pin, roll out dough to an 8-inch circle. Using a 1½-inch round cutter, cut 10 rounds from each dough portion, rerolling scraps as necessary. Place dough rounds 2 inches apart on prepared baking sheets.
• Bake for 6 minutes. Remove from oven, and let cool on wire racks. Once cooled, cake rounds can be stored with layers separated by wax paper in an airtight container in a cool, dry place for up to 3 days before serving.
• Spread 1½ teaspoons Sour Cream Frosting onto each cake layer. Carefully stack 5 layers for each cake to make 8 cake stacks. Place cake stacks on a rimmed baking sheet, and freeze for 30 minutes.
• Spread a thin layer Sour Cream Frosting on top and sides of cake stacks. Freeze for 30 minutes. Repeat procedure twice. Refrigerate finished cakes for at least 24 hours before serving.
• Garnish with Chocolate Bees, if desired.

MAKE-AHEAD TIP: Cakes can be assembled, frosted, stored in an airtight container, and frozen up to a day in advance. Let thaw for 40 minutes in refrigerator before serving.

Sour Cream Frosting
Makes 4 cups

½ cup heavy whipping cream
2 cups sour cream
1½ cups confectioners' sugar

• In the bowl of a stand mixer fitted with the whisk attachment, beat cream at high speed until stiff peaks form, 1 to 2 minutes.
• In a large bowl, whisk together sour cream and confectioners' sugar. Fold whipped cream into sour cream mixture. Refrigerate until ready to use.

Chocolate Bees
Makes 8

¼ cup dark chocolate melting wafers*
½ cup white chocolate melting wafers*
1 drop yellow food coloring
8 sliced almonds, halved

• In a medium microwave-safe bowl, melt dark chocolate wafers on high in 30-second intervals, stirring between each, until smooth.
• Transfer melted dark chocolate to a paper piping bag with a small hole cut at tip. Pipe 8 (¼-inch) oval dots of dark chocolate onto a nonstick baking mat. Let cool completely.
• In a medium microwave-safe bowl, melt white chocolate wafers on high in 30-second intervals, stirring between each, until smooth. Add yellow food coloring, stirring until desired color is achieved.
• Transfer melted white chocolate mixture to a paper piping bag with a small hole cut at tip. Pipe 3 to 5 stripes onto dark chocolate ovals to create bumble bee stripes.
• Pipe a thin layer of dark chocolate onto cut end of each almond slice half. Press an almond slice half onto each side of chocolate bees to create wings. (Melted dark chocolate will serve as the glue.) Hold wings in place until dark chocolate "glue" sets. Store in an airtight container in a cool, dark place until ready to use.

*We used Ghirardelli Melting Wafers.

Scotland

The Scotts are credited with inventing the scone in the 16th century, and the tradition of afternoon tea is widely attributed to the English, particularly to Anna Maria Stanhope Russell, the seventh Duchess of Bedford. In the 19th century, dinner was typically served late in the day, sometime after 7:00 p.m. A lady-in-waiting to Queen Victoria in the 1840s, Lady Bedford reportedly began having a light snack along with a cup of tea around 4:00 p.m., and soon started inviting friends to join her, inspiring others to adopt the practice. While small sandwiches, biscuits (cookies), and cakes may have been the norm for teatime, scones didn't become foundational to afternoon tea until the 20th century.

Enjoy a menu of teatime favorites from the highlands of Scotland, such as bridies filled with steak and onion and a clever variation on Scotch eggs. Here, the word "scone" rhymes with gone, shortbread is considered the crown jewel of Scottish baking, and tea is black and strong. Savor this bonnie afternoon tea from thistle-embellished china set atop a table clad with touches of plaid.

The MENU

SAVORIES
Steak & Onion Bridies
Scotch Egg Canapés
Smoked Trout Tea Sandwiches
Scottish Breakfast

SCONE
Oat & Wheat Scones
Earl Grey

SWEETS
Dundee Cake
Lemon-Vanilla Shortbread
Raspberry-Oat Tartlets
with Whiskey-Honey Cream
Victorian Afternoon

Tea Pairings by Mark T. Wendell Tea Company,
978-635-9200, marktwendell.com

Steak & Onion Bridies
Makes 16

1 tablespoon olive oil
½ pound ground sirloin
½ cup finely chopped yellow onion
1 (10.5-ounce) can beef consommé
½ cup very small diced russet potato
1 teaspoon fresh thyme leaves
1 teaspoon dry mustard
¼ teaspoon ground black pepper
2 (17.3-ounce) packages frozen puff pastry, thawed
1 large egg
1 tablespoon water
Garnish: fresh thyme leaves

• Preheat oven to 400°. Line 2 rimmed baking sheets with parchment paper.
• In a medium sauté pan, heat oil over medium-high heat until shimmering. Add sirloin and onion; cook, stirring frequently, until sirloin is browned and onion is tender. Add consommé, potato, thyme, mustard, and pepper; reduce heat to medium-low. Cover and cook, stirring frequently, until potato is tender and mixture is heated through, 5 to 7 minutes. Uncover and cook until liquid is gone. Remove from heat, and let cool to room temperature.
• On a lightly floured surface, unroll puff pastry sheets. Using a rolling pin, roll each sheet to a ¼-inch thickness. Using a 4-inch round cutter, cut 16 rounds from sheets. Place approximately 1 tablespoon sirloin mixture in center of each pastry round.
• In a small bowl, whisk together egg and 1 tablespoon water. Using a pastry brush, coat edges of pastry rounds with egg wash. Fold pastry rounds in half to encase sirloin mixture, and crimp edges with a fork. Place bridies on prepared baking sheets. Brush pastries with remaining egg wash. Garnish bridies with thyme leaves, if desired.
• Bake until bridies are golden brown, approximately 15 minutes. Serve warm.

Scotch Egg Canapés
Makes 8

3 slices firm white sandwich bread, frozen
8 ounces ground pork breakfast sausage
½ cup all-purpose flour
2 large eggs, beaten
½ cup fine bread crumbs
1 cup vegetable oil
3 slices medium Cheddar cheese
3 medium hard-cooked eggs, peeled
¼ cup prepared piccalilli

• Preheat oven to 350°. Line a rimmed baking sheet with parchment paper.
• Using a 1¾-inch round cutter, cut 8 rounds from frozen bread slices. Place on prepared baking sheet.
• Bake until bread slices are crisp and light golden brown, 7 to 10 minutes. Let cool completely.
• Line a rimmed baking sheet with wax paper.
• Divide sausage into 8 golf-ball-size balls. Press flat onto prepared baking sheet. Freeze for 10 to 15 minutes.
• Remove sausage patties from freezer, and dredge in flour, beaten eggs, and bread crumbs to coat.
• In a medium sauté pan, heat oil over medium-high heat until shimmering. Fry sausage patties until crumb coating is light golden brown, approximately 1 minute per side. Let drain on paper towels.
• Line a rimmed baking sheet with parchment paper. Place sausage patties on prepared baking sheet.
• Bake until interiors of sausage patties are cooked, 5 to 7 minutes.
• Using a 1¾-inch round cutter, cut each sausage patty to neaten edges, discarding scraps. Using the same cutter, cut 8 rounds from cheese slices, discarding scraps.
• Using an egg slicer, slice boiled eggs horizontally into thin slices.
• Spread piccalilli onto toasted bread rounds. Top each with a sausage patty, a cheese round, and an egg slice. Serve immediately.

Smoked Trout Tea Sandwiches
Makes 6

1 (8-ounce) package lemon pepper and garlic smoked trout fillet
½ cup mayonnaise
1 tablespoon creamy prepared horseradish
1 tablespoon finely snipped fresh dill
1 teaspoon fresh lemon zest
⅛ teaspoon ground black pepper
4 slices large firm whole-grain white sandwich bread
6 thin horizontal slices English cucumber

• Remove and discard skin from trout. Rinse excess spice from trout, and pat dry. Flake trout into a medium bowl. Add mayonnaise, horseradish, dill, lemon zest, and pepper, stirring to combine. Spread mixture onto 2 bread slices. Cover with remaining 2 bread slices. Using a serrated bread knife, trim crusts from sandwiches. Cut each sandwich into 3 rectangles.
• Remove top bread slices from each tea sandwich. Place a cucumber slice on each tea sandwich, and trim to fit. Replace top bread slices. Serve immediately, or cover with damp paper towels, place in a covered container, and refrigerate until serving time.

• Red Currant Jam • Clotted Cream

time.) Working gently, bring mixture together with hands until a dough forms.
• Turn out dough onto a lightly floured surface, and knead gently 4 to 5 times. Using a rolling pin, roll out dough to a ¾-inch thickness. Using a 2-inch square cutter, cut 12 scones from dough. Place scones 2 inches apart on prepared baking sheet. Brush tops of scones with remaining 1 tablespoon cold cream.
• Bake until edges of scones are golden brown and a wooden pick inserted in centers comes out clean, approximately 12 minutes. Serve warm.

Dundee Cake
Makes 1 (8-inch) cake

1 cup very hot water
1 cup golden raisins
1 cup salted butter, softened
¾ cup granulated sugar
4 large eggs
2 large egg yolks
1 teaspoon vanilla extract
1⅔ cups all-purpose flour
1 tablespoon orange zest
2 teaspoons baking powder
½ teaspoon salt
½ teaspoon ground allspice
1 cup dried chopped pineapple
½ cup dried chopped dates
Garnish: confectioners' sugar

• Preheat oven to 325°. Spray an 8-inch springform pan with baking spray with flour.
• In a small bowl, pour 1 cup very hot water over raisins. Let stand for 15 minutes. Drain well.
• In a large bowl, beat together butter and granulated sugar with a mixer at medium speed until light and creamy, 4 to 5 minutes. Add eggs and then egg yolks, one at a time, beating well after each addition. Add vanilla extract, beating to combine.
• In a medium bowl, whisk together flour, orange zest, baking powder, salt, and allspice. With mixer on low speed, gradually add flour mixture to butter mixture, beating until incorporated. Add raisins, pineapple, and dates, beating until just combined.
• Spread batter into prepared pan, smoothing top with an offset spatula. Tap pan on counter to level and settle batter.
• Bake until cake is golden brown and a wooden pick inserted in center comes out clean, 1 hour to 1 hour and 15 minutes. Let cool in pan for 10 minutes. Remove sides of pan, and let cool completely on a wire rack. Slide cake off bottom of springform pan onto a cake plate before serving.
• Garnish with confectioners' sugar, if desired.

Oat & Wheat Scones
Makes 12

1 cup whole wheat flour
½ cup all-purpose flour
½ cup quick-cooking oats
⅓ cup firmly packed light brown sugar
2 teaspoons baking powder
½ teaspoon salt
6 tablespoons cold salted butter, cubed
½ cup plus 3 tablespoons cold heavy whipping cream, divided
1 large egg

• Preheat oven to 400°. Line a rimmed baking sheet with parchment paper.
• In a large bowl, whisk together flours, oats, brown sugar, baking powder, and salt. Using a pastry blender or 2 forks, cut in cold butter until mixture resembles coarse crumbs.
• In a liquid-measuring cup, whisk together ½ cup plus 2 tablespoons cold cream and egg. Add cream mixture to flour mixture, stirring until mixture is evenly moist. (If dough seems dry, add more cream, 1 tablespoon at a

Lemon-Vanilla Shortbread
Makes 8 wedges

½ cup salted butter, softened
½ cup confectioners' sugar
1 teaspoon fresh lemon zest
½ teaspoon lemon extract
½ teaspoon vanilla extract
1 cup all-purpose flour
⅛ teaspoon salt

• Preheat oven to 325°. Lightly spray an 8-inch shortbread pan* with cooking spray.
• In a large bowl, beat butter with a mixer at medium speed until creamy. Add confectioners' sugar, lemon zest, lemon extract, and vanilla extract, beating to blend. Add flour and salt, beating until incorporated.
• Firmly press dough into prepared pan. Prick dough with a fork.
• Bake until shortbread is light golden brown, approximately 35 minutes. Let cool in pan for 10 minutes. Turn out shortbread onto a cutting board. Cut into wedges to serve.

We used an 8-inch hexagonal Scottish thistle ceramic shortbread pan from Brown Bag Designs, shortbreadpan.com. Shortbread can also be baked in an 8-inch round cake pan.

Raspberry-Oat Tartlets with Whiskey-Honey Cream
Makes 6

1½ cups oat and honey granola cereal
¼ cup granulated sugar
¼ cup salted butter, melted
1 cup heavy whipping cream
½ cup sour cream
1 tablespoon Scotch whiskey
2 tablespoons honey, divided
Fresh raspberries

• Preheat oven to 350°.
• In the work bowl of a food processor, combine granola and sugar; pulse until finely chopped. Reserve 1 tablespoon granola crumbs for topping.
• In a medium bowl, stir together granola crumb mixture and melted butter. Divide mixture among 6 (4-inch) removable-bottom tartlet pans. Firmly press mixture into bottoms and up sides of tartlet pans. Place tartlet pans on a rimmed baking sheet. Freeze for 15 minutes.
• Bake for 10 minutes. Let crusts cool completely before removing from tartlet pans.

• In a medium bowl, beat cream with a mixer at high speed until soft peaks form. Slowly add sour cream, whiskey, and 1 tablespoon honey, beating until incorporated.
• Divide cream mixture among tartlet crusts. Top with raspberries. Drizzle with remaining 1 tablespoon honey. Top with reserved 1 tablespoon granola crumbs.

We used Dewar's White Label Scotch Whiskey.

South Africa

South Africa's rooibos (meaning "red bush") has made a name for itself in the global beverage industry. While it doesn't come from the *Camellia sinesis* and, therefore, isn't technically tea, the herbal brew is popular for its earthy yet sweet flavor, vibrant color, and lack of caffeine. Rooibos and its cousin honeybush are grown in the mountainous region just north of Cape Town. Both herbs became popular in the early 18th century when Dutch settlers began to brew them as less expensive alternatives to black tea.

In addition to Dutch influences on South African tea culture, there have been British ones. Teatime fare typically follows the British order of tea sandwiches, scones, and desserts. This South African-inspired menu celebrates the country's contributions to culinary culture by including savory dishes that feature lamb and mackerel, a scone infused with honeybush, and sweets, such as malva pudding cakes that incorporate rooibos. A simple, yet eye-catching table with multicolored china and cheery flowers pays tribute to the beautiful nation of South Africa.

The
MENU

SAVORIES
Mackerel and Corn
Stuffed Peppers
Tamatiebredie (Lamb Stew)
Braaibroodjie (Cheese, Grilled
Onion and Tomato Panini)
Organic African Outback Rooibos

SCONE
Honeybush Scones
Cederburg Harvest Green Rooibos

SWEETS
Rooibos-Infused
Malva Pudding Cakes
Milk Tartlets
Chocolate & Pepper Cookies
Dragonfruit Rooibos

Tea Pairings by Simpson & Vail,
800-282-8327, svtea.com

Mackerel and Corn Stuffed Peppers
Makes 8

8 assorted baby bell peppers
1 tablespoon unsalted butter
2 cups fresh yellow corn kernels
1 tablespoon chopped fresh parsley
1 tablespoon chopped green onion tops
1 teaspoon chopped fresh thyme
½ teaspoon salt
½ teaspoon hot sauce*
¼ teaspoon granulated sugar
⅛ teaspoon ground black pepper
1 (4.375-ounce) can skinless boneless
    mackerel fillets in olive oil
½ cup panko (Japanese bread crumbs)
2 tablespoons unsalted butter, melted
¼ teaspoon chili powder

• Preheat oven to 375º.
• Fill a medium saucepan with water, and heat over high heat until boiling.
• Using a sharp knife, cut tops from bell peppers, and remove and discard seeds and membranes. Place peppers in boiling water. Boil gently for 5 minutes. Remove, and drain well.
• Place peppers upright in a baking dish for stuffing. (If necessary, trim bottom rounded edges slightly to level.)
• In a medium sauté pan, melt butter over medium-high heat. Add corn, parsley, green onion tops, thyme, salt, hot sauce, sugar, and black pepper; cook for 1 to 2 minutes, stirring constantly. Remove from heat.
• Flake mackerel into small pieces. Add mackerel to corn mixture, stirring to combine.
• Divide corn mixture among peppers, stuffing well.
• In a small bowl, stir together bread crumbs, melted butter, and chili powder. Sprinkle mixture on top of stuffed peppers.
• Bake until bread crumbs are browned, 7 to 10 minutes. Serve warm.

*We used Tabasco sauce.

Tamatiebredie (Lamb Stew)
Makes 8 servings

1 tablespoon unsalted butter
1 tablespoon olive oil
1 cup chopped yellow onion
1 pound ground lamb
1 tablespoon finely chopped garlic
2 teaspoons chili powder
1 teaspoon salt

½ teaspoon ground black pepper
1 (14.5-ounce) can petite diced tomatoes
1 (6-ounce) can tomato paste
1 cup water
1 tablespoon distilled white vinegar
1 teaspoon firmly packed light brown sugar
1 bay leaf
6 boiled petite honey gold potatoes, peeled and diced
2 cups hot cooked basmati rice
Garnish: chopped fresh parsley

• In a medium Dutch oven or saucepan, heat butter and oil over medium-high heat until butter melts. Add onion; reduce heat to medium-low. Cook, stirring occasionally, until onion is very tender and a light gold color. Add lamb, garlic, chili powder, salt, and pepper; increase heat to medium. Cook, stirring occasionally, until lamb is no longer pink. Add tomatoes, tomato paste, 1 cup water, vinegar, brown sugar, and bay leaf; cook, stirring occasionally, until mixture comes to a boil. Reduce heat to low; cover and cook for 1 hour.
• Add potatoes to stew; cook until potatoes are tender. Remove bay leaf.
• To serve, spoon ½ cup stew over a ¼ cup hot cooked rice.
• Garnish with parsley, if desired.

MAKE-AHEAD TIP: Stew may be made without potatoes a day in advance, stored in a covered container, and refrigerated. Reheat, add potatoes, and cook until potatoes are tender.

discarding crusts. Cut each sandwich diagonally into 4 triangles. Serve warm.

We used Mrs. H.S. Ball's Chutney, an iconic Cape Town chutney, available at World Market.

Honeybush Scones
Makes 9

3 tablespoons plus 1½ teaspoons loose-leaf
  (7 tea bags) honeybush, divided
1¼ cups heavy whipping cream
½ teaspoon vanilla extract
2 cups all-purpose flour
⅓ cup plus 1 tablespoon granulated sugar, divided
1 tablespoon baking powder
½ teaspoon salt
¼ cup cold unsalted butter

• If using loose-leaf, place 3 tablespoons honeybush in a fine-mesh infuser basket, and set infuser basket in a heatproof bowl, or if using tea bags, place 6 tea bags in a heatproof bowl.
• In a small saucepan, heat cream until very hot, but not boiling. Pour over honeybush. Let steep and come to room temperature. Cover and refrigerate overnight.
• Remove infuser basket or tea bags from steeped cream, pressing or squeezing to remove excess liquid from honeybush. Discard honeybush. Transfer steeped cream to a 1-cup or larger liquid-measuring cup. (If steeped cream is less than 1 cup, add plain cold heavy whipping cream to steeped cream to equal 1 cup.) Add vanilla extract, stirring well.
• Preheat oven to 350°. Line a rimmed baking sheet with parchment paper.
• In a large bowl, whisk together flour, ⅓ cup sugar, baking powder, salt, and remaining 1½ teaspoons honeybush. Using a pastry blender or 2 forks, cut in cold butter until it resembles coarse crumbs. Add ¾ cup cream mixture to flour mixture, stirring until evenly moist. (If dough seems dry, add more cream mixture, 1 tablespoon at a time.) Working gently, bring mixture together with hands until a dough forms.
• Turn out dough onto a lightly floured surface, and knead gently 4 to 5 times. Using a rolling pin, roll out dough to a ¾-inch thickness. Using a 2¼-inch round cutter, cut 9 scones from dough, rerolling scraps as necessary. Place scones 2 inches apart on prepared baking sheet. Brush top of scones with any remaining cream mixture, and sprinkle with remaining 1 tablespoon sugar.
• Bake until edges of scones are golden brown and a wooden pick inserted in centers comes out clean, approximately 20 minutes. Serve warm.

Braaibroodjie (Cheese, Grilled Onion and Tomato Panini)
Makes 8

1 teaspoon olive oil
4 green onions, trimmed and halved lengthwise
1 cup coarsely grated sharp white Cheddar cheese,
  divided
4 very large slices firm white bread
1 medium tomato, thinly sliced
⅛ teaspoon salt
⅛ teaspoon ground black pepper
3 tablespoons peach-apricot chutney*
¼ cup salted butter, softened

• In a large nonstick sauté pan, heat oil over medium-high heat until it shimmers. Add green onions; cook, turning once, until each side is slightly charred and still green, 1 to 2 minutes per side. Remove green onions, and let cool. Coarsely chop, and set aside.
• Sprinkle ½ cup cheese onto 2 bread slices. Place 2 tomato slices over cheese on each bread slice. Sprinkle with salt, pepper, and chopped green onions. Sprinkle with remaining ½ cup cheese. Spread an even layer of chutney onto remaining 2 bread slices, and place on top of cheese, chutney side down. Spread butter onto each bread slice.
• Heat a large nonstick pan or griddle over medium-high heat. Cook sandwiches until golden brown on both sides and cheese melts, reducing heat, if necessary. Transfer sandwiches to a cutting surface, and let cool slightly.
• Using a long serrated bread knife and a gentle sawing motion, cut each sandwich into a 2¼-inch square,

RECOMMENDED
CONDIMENTS

• Orange Marmalade
• Cream

Rooibos-Infused Malva Pudding Cakes

Makes 36

3 tablespoons loose-leaf (6 tea bags) rooibos
1 cup whole milk
1 large egg
1 cup granulated sugar
3 tablespoons apricot preserves
1 cup all-purpose flour
1 teaspoon baking soda
⅛ teaspoon salt
1 tablespoon unsalted butter, melted
1 teaspoon apple cider vinegar
Toffee Sauce (recipe follows)

• If using loose-leaf, place rooibos in a fine-mesh infuser basket, and set infuser basket in a heatproof bowl, or if using tea bags, place 6 tea bags in a heatproof bowl.
• In a small saucepan, heat milk until very hot, but not boiling. Pour over rooibos. Cover and let steep for 15 minutes. Remove infuser basket or tea bags from steeped milk, pressing or squeezing to remove excess liquid from rooibos. Discard rooibos. Let steeped milk come to room temperature.
• Preheat oven to 350°. Spray a 9-inch square baking pan with cooking spray.
• In a large bowl, beat together egg and sugar with a mixer at medium speed until very pale in color and mixture has increased in volume, 2 to 3 minutes. Add preserves, beating until incorporated.
• In a medium bowl, whisk together flour, baking soda, and salt.
• In a small bowl, stir together melted butter and vinegar. Add butter mixture to steeped milk, stirring well. With mixer at low speed, gradually add milk mixture to egg mixture alternately with flour mixture, beginning and ending with milk mixture, beating just until combined after each addition. Transfer batter to prepared baking pan. Cover pan with foil.
• Bake until cake is browned and a wooden pick inserted in center comes out clean, approximately 35 minutes. Immediately pour Toffee Sauce over warm cake. Let stand for sauce to be absorbed into cake.
• Using a sharp knife, cut into 36 (1¼-inch) squares. Serve warm or at room temperature.

Toffee Sauce

Makes 1¼ cups

½ cup unsalted butter
¾ cup heavy whipping cream
½ cup granulated sugar
⅓ cup water
⅛ teaspoon salt

• In a medium saucepan, melt butter over medium-low heat. Add cream, sugar, ⅓ cup water, and salt, stirring to combine. Cook until sugar dissolves and mixture is creamy. Use immediately.

Milk Tartlets

Makes 16

2 (14.1-ounce) packages refrigerated piecrusts
½ cup granulated sugar
¼ cup cake flour
3 tablespoons cornstarch
⅛ teaspoon salt
3 cups whole milk, divided
½ cup unsalted butter, cubed
4 large eggs, separated
½ teaspoon vanilla extract
Garnish: cinnamon sugar

• Preheat oven to 400°. Lightly spray 16 deep (4-inch) tartlet pans with cooking spray.
• Using a rolling pin, unroll piecrusts on a lightly floured surface. Using a 3¼-inch round cutter, cut 16 rounds from dough. Press into prepared tartlet pans, trimming excess dough from tops. Using the large end of a chopstick, press dough into indentations in sides of tartlet pans. Prick bottom of crusts with a fork to prevent puffing. Place tartlet pans on a rimmed baking sheet. Freeze for 15 minutes.
• Bake until very light golden brown, approximately 7 minutes. Let cool completely. Reduce oven temperature to 375°.
• In a medium bowl, whisk together granulated sugar, flour, cornstarch, and salt. Gradually add ½ cup milk, whisking until smooth.
• In a medium saucepan, heat remaining 2½ cups milk over medium-high heat until very hot, but not boiling. Remove from heat. Add sugar mixture to hot milk, whisking until incorporated. Return saucepan to heat, and cook over medium heat, whisking constantly, until mixture thickens. Remove from heat. Gradually add butter, whisking until combined.
• Using a fork, beat egg yolks. Add beaten eggs to custard mixture, whisking well. Add vanilla extract, whisking until combined.
• In a large bowl, beat egg whites with a mixer at high speed until stiff peaks form. Using a spatula, gently fold beaten egg whites into custard. Divide custard among prepared tartlet shells.
• Bake until tartlets are slightly puffed, 13 to 15 minutes. Let cool slightly before carefully removing from pans. (Tartlets will fall when cool.) Serve warm, cold, or at room temperature.
• Garnish tartlets with a sprinkle of cinnamon sugar, if desired.

Chocolate & Pepper Cookies

Makes 90

1 cup unsalted butter, softened
¾ cup granulated sugar
¾ cup dark muscovado sugar*
2 large eggs
1 teaspoon vanilla extract
2¼ cups all-purpose flour
1 teaspoon baking soda
1 teaspoon freshly ground black pepper
1 teaspoon ground black pepper
½ teaspoon salt
2 (4-ounce) bars bittersweet chocolate, melted and cooled
1 (12-ounce) package semisweet chocolate morsels
Garnish: Maldon salt flakes

• Preheat oven to 375°. Line several rimmed baking sheets with parchment paper.
• In a large bowl, beat together butter and sugars with a mixer at medium speed until light and fluffy, 3 to 4 minutes, stopping to scrape sides of bowl. Add eggs, beating well. Add vanilla extract, beating until incorporated.
• In a medium bowl, whisk together flour, baking soda, peppers, and salt. With mixer on low speed, gradually add flour mixture to butter mixture, beating until combined. Add melted chocolate, beating until incorporated. Add chocolate morsels, stirring well.
• Using a levered 2-teaspoon scoop, portion dough and place 2 inches apart on prepared baking sheets.
• Garnish cookie dough with a sprinkle of salt flakes, if desired.
• Bake until cookies are dark brown and set, 8 to 10 minutes. Remove cookies from baking sheets, and let cool completely on wire racks. Store in a covered container with layers separated by wax paper until ready to serve.

*Dark muscovado sugar is from Mauritius off the coast of Africa, available through India Tree Gourmet Spices & Specialities, indiatree.com.

EDITOR'S NOTE: In order to achieve a nice balance of flavors, we recommend using 1 teaspoon freshly ground pepper from a grinder as well as 1 teaspoon pre-ground pepper. While these amounts might seem excessive, they are needed for this recipe.

HOW TO MAKE
TARTLET CRUST

on page 131

TEA-STEEPING *Guide*

The quality of the tea served at afternoon tea is as important as the food and the décor. To be sure your infusion is successful every time, here are some basic guidelines to follow.

WATER

Always use the best water possible. If the water tastes good, so will your tea. Heat the water on the stove top or in an electric kettle to the desired temperature. A microwave oven is not recommended.

TEMPERATURE

Heating the water to the correct temperature is arguably one of the most important factors in making a great pot of tea. Pouring boiling water on green, white, or oolong tea leaves can result in a very unpleasant brew. Always refer to the tea purveyor's packaging for specific instructions, but in general, use 170° to 195° water for these delicate tea types. Reserve boiling (212°) water for black and puerh teas, as well as herbal and fruit tisanes.

TEAPOT

If the teapot you plan to use is delicate, warm it with hot tap water first to avert possible cracking. Discard this water before adding the tea leaves or tea bags.

TEA

Use the highest-quality tea you can afford, whether loose leaf or prepackaged in bags or sachets. Remember that these better teas can often be steeped more than once. When using loose-leaf tea, generally use 1 generous teaspoon of dry leaf per 8 ounces of water, and use an infuser basket. For a stronger infusion, add another teaspoonful or two of dry tea leaf.

TIME

As soon as the water reaches the correct temperature for the type of tea, pour it over the leaves or tea bag in the teapot, and cover the pot with a lid. Set a timer—usually 1 to 2 minutes for whites and oolongs; 2 to 3 minutes for greens; and 3 to 5 minutes for blacks, puerhs, and herbals. (Steeping tea longer than recommended can yield a bitter infusion.) When the timer goes off, remove the infuser basket or the tea bags from the teapot.

ENJOYMENT

For best flavor, serve the tea as soon as possible. Keep the beverage warm atop a lighted warmer or under your favorite tea cozy if necessary.

Let these step-by-step photos serve as your visual guide while
you create these impressive and delicious teatime treats.

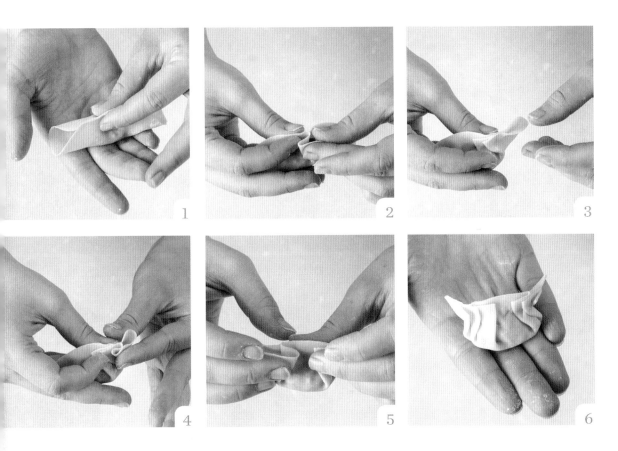

Pot Stickers (page 29) 1 Fold wrapper in half, pinching together at middle. 2 Make a pleat in the upper edge
of the wrapper just to left of center. 3 Make another pleat in wrapper just to the left of the first pleat. 4 Make a third
pleat in wrapper just to the left of the second pleat. 5 Make a pleat in the upper edge of the wrapper just to the right
of center. 6 Make two more pleats as before to seal right edge.

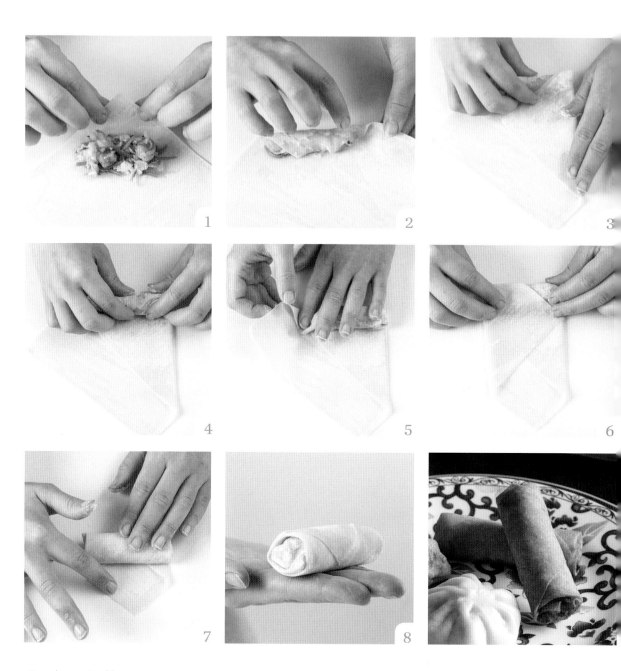

Spring Rolls (page 25)
1 Place a spring roll wrapper, shiny side down with a corner pointed toward you. Place 1 to 1½ tablespoons filling on corner closest to you.   2 Fold corner tightly over filling.   3 Fold left side in tightly, making sure not to leave any space.   4 Roll once away from you.   5 Fold right side in tightly.   6 Roll again, keeping edges straight and even, until you reach top corner.   7 Using your fingertip, brush edges of top corner with cornstarch mixture.   8 Fold top corner to close roll.

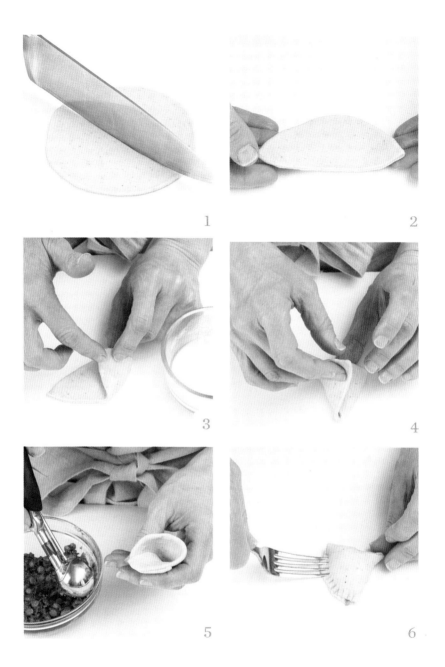

Samosa (page 52)   1 Using a sharp knife, cut dough circle in half to create 2 semicircles. 2 Work with one semicircle at a time and keep rounded edge toward you.   3 Fold left corner toward center, and brush flour paste on folded left side.   4 Fold right side over left to form a triangle, and press gently until sides stick.   5 Open dough triangle gently to form a cone, and fill with lentil mixture, being careful not to overfill.   6 Spread flour paste onto top edges of cone. Using a fork, seal top edges of cone, enclosing filling.

Pavlovas (page 16) 1 Line a baking sheet with parchment paper. Trace 2-inch circles onto parchment. Flip parchment over. 2 Working from the center outward, pipe concentric circles of meringue mixture until circle is filled. 3 Pipe 1 to 2 extra layers onto perimeters of rounds to form a rim around the edge of each circle. 4 Repeat piping procedure to fill all traced circles. Bake according to recipe.

Tartlet Crust (page 122) 1 Using a cutter, cut shapes from dough. 2 Press dough shapes into tartlet pans. 3 Trim excess dough. 4 Using the wide end of a chopstick, push dough into indentations of pan.

Acknowledgments

COVER

Photography by John O'Hagan
Recipe Development and Food Styling by Janet Lambert / Styling by Courtni Bodiford
Bernardaud *Siècle* salad plate, teacup and saucer set, teapot, 3-tiered stand, and rectangular cake platter, 212-371-4300, *bernardaud.com*. Flower arrangement*.

AUSTRALIA

Photography by Jim Bathie
Recipe Development and Food Styling by Janet Lambert / Styling by Courtni Bodiford
Pages 10–19: 222 Fifth *Adelaide* dinner plate, salad plate, teacup/saucer set, teapot, creamer, sugar, oval platter, and 2-tiered stand; Oneida *Satinike* knife, salad fork, and teaspoon[†]. Natural Fiber place mat[‡]. Isaac Mizrahi condiment bowl set from Gibson Outlet, 800-281-2810, *gibsonusaoutlet.com*.

CHINA

Photography by William Dickey
Recipe Development and Food Styling by Laura Crandall / Styling by Courtni Bodiford
Pages 20–31: Mottahedeh *Blue Canton* dinner plate, bread and butter plate, teacup/saucer set, teapot, creamer, sugar bowl, rectangular platter, and platter with metal handle from Mottahedeh, 800-443-8225, *mottahedeh.com*. Ralph Lauren *Mandarin Blue* salad plate, teapot, creamer, sugar, small square dish, oval bowl, and rectangular platter[†]. Table runner from Cotton and Quill, 205-848-2785, *cottonandquill.com*.

FRANCE

Photography by William Dickey and John O'Hagan / Recipe Development and Food Styling by Janet Lambert Styling by Courtni Bodiford
Pages 32–45: Bernardaud *Siècle* dinner plate, salad plate, bread and butter plate, teacup and saucer set, teapot, creamer, sugar, 3-tiered stand, rectangular cake platter, footed cake stand, and tart platter, 212-371-4300, *bernardaud.com*. Vietri *Rufolo Gold* charger and Garnier Thiebaut *Eloise* napkin from Bromberg's, 205-871-3276, *brombergs.com*. Towle *French Provincial* knife and Christofle *Marly* fork and teaspoon[†]. Flower arrangement*.

INDIA

Photography by William Dickey
Recipe Development and Food Styling by Vanessa Rocchio / Styling by Courtni Bodiford
Pages 46–55: Philippe Deshoulières *Dhara* dinner plate, bread and butter plate, teapot, creamer, sugar, round cake platter, round platter, footed candy tray, and rectangular tray from FX Dougherty, 800-834-3797, *fxdougherty.com*. Royal Worcester *Carnation* salad plate; Royal Doulton *Napier* teacup/saucer set; Geneve *Golden Barclay* flatware available for rent from Tea and Old Roses, 205-413-7753, *teaandoldroses.com*. Rose Pink and Golden Whipstitch napkin from Pier 1 Imports, 817-252-6300, *pier1.com*.

JAPAN

Photography by Marcy Black Simpson
Recipe Development and Food Styling by Jade Sinacori/Styling by Courtni Bodiford
Pages 56–67: Royal Crown Derby *Traditional Imari* dinner plate, teacup and saucer set, bouillon cup and saucer set, teapot, oval platter, handled cake/pastry plate, and small oval duchess sweet bowl[†]. *Indigo Organic Reactive Glaze* salad plate; *Gold Wave* flatware; crafted chopsticks; napkin ring; Fiber Lurex table runner and place mat[‡].

MOROCCO

Photography by John O'Hagan
Recipe Development and Food Styling by Janet Lambert / Styling by Courtni Bodiford
Pages 68–79: *Essaouira* tea glasses; clear glass teapot; tagine; silver tray from Casablanca Market, 650-964-3000, *casablancamarket.com*. Wedgwood *Ascot* dinner plate; Christian Dior *Tabriz* salad plate; Towle *El Grandee* flatware[†]. Napkin ring from Pier 1 Imports, 817-252-6300, *pier1.com*. Lanterns[‡]. Location courtesy of Gabrella Manor, Birmingham, Alabama, 205-833-9754, *gabrellamanor.com*.

NETHERLANDS

Photography by William Dickey
Recipe Development and Food Styling by Janet Lambert / Styling by Courtni Bodiford
Pages 80–89: DeWit Handpainted Delftware *Windmill* dessert plate, teacup and saucer set; *Poly Flower* teapot, creamer and sugar set, deep plate, and vase; *Blue Flower* pedestal stand; *Blue Mill* pedestal stand and appliqué from Dutch Village, 616-396-1475, *dutchvillage.com*. Oneida *Cantata* flatware[†]. Juliska *Sitio Stripe Indigo* dinner plate from Bromberg's, 205-871-3276, *brombergs.com*.

RUSSIA

Photography by Caroline Smith
Recipe Development and Food Styling by Jade Sinacori / Styling by Courtni Bodiford
Pages 90–101: Mikasa *Wedding Band Gold* salad plate; Lomonosov *Winding Twig* bread and butter plate; Lomonosov *Cobalt Net* dinner plate, teapot, creamer, sugar, teacup/saucer, round dish, oval platter, and compote; Gorham *Fairfax* flatware[†]. Samovar set from St. Petersburg Store, 800-531-1037, *fromrussia.com*. Mother-of-pearl spoon from Table Matters, 205-879-0125, *table-matters.com*. Gold soup bowl[†]. Flower arrangement*.

SCOTLAND

Photography by John O'Hagan
Recipe Development and Food Styling by Janet Lambert / Styling by Lucy W. Herndon
Pages 102–111: Royal Albert *Brigadoon* dinner plate, salad plate, footed cup and saucer, teapot, oval platter, creamer, and sugar bowl[†]. Mikasa *Regent Bead* flatware from Mikasa, 866-645-2721, *mikasa.com*. Shell sugar tongs from Tea for Two, 949-855-1380, *teafortwo.com*. Rosanna *Le Gateau* pedestal from Rosanna, Inc., 877-343-3779, *rosannainc.com*. Flower arrangement*.

SOUTH AFRICA

Photography by Marcy Black Simpson
Recipe Development and Food Styling by Janet Lambert / Styling by Courtni Bodiford
Pages 112–123: Gien *Eden* teacup and saucer set, teapot, creamer, sugar bowl, square platter, and rectangular platter[†]. World Market *Verde* dinner plate; *Amber* salad plate; Khadi *Melange* table runner[‡]. Flower arrangement*.

BACK COVER

Photography by William Dickey
Recipe Development and Food Styling by Janet Lambert / Styling by Courtni Bodiford
Bernardaud *Siècle* teacup and saucer set, footed cake stand, 212-371-4300, *bernardaud.com*.

* *From FlowerBuds, 205-970-3223, flowerbudsfloristbirmingham.com*
[†] *From Replacements, Ltd., 800-737-5223, replacements.com.*
[‡] *From World Market, 877-967-5362, worldmarket.com*

EDITOR'S NOTE: *Items not listed are from private collections. Unfortunately, no pattern or manufacturer information is available.*

Recipe INDEX

EDITOR'S NOTE: Recipe titles shown in blue are gluten-free, provided gluten-free versions of processed ingredients (such as flours, extracts, crackers, breads, and broths) are used.

"Come, let us have some tea and continue to talk about happy things."

—Chaim Potok